Biting through the Skin

Biting through the Skin

*An Indian Kitchen in
America's Heartland*

NINA MUKERJEE FURSTENAU

University of Iowa Press, Iowa City

University of Iowa Press, Iowa City 52242
Copyright © 2013 by Nina Mukerjee Furstenau
www.uiowapress.org
Printed in the United States of America

Design by Ashley Muehlbauer

The University of Iowa Press is a member of Green
Press Initiative and is committed to preserving natu-
ral resources.

Printed on acid-free paper

Library of Congress Cataloging-in-Publication Data
Furstenau, Nina Mukerjee, 1962–
Biting through the skin: an Indian kitchen in
America's heartland / by Nina Mukerjee Furstenau.
pages   cm.
ISBN 978-1-60938-185-1, 1-60938-185-8 (pbk.)
ISBN 978-1-60938-208-7, 1-60938-208-0 (ebook)
1. Furstenau, Nina Mukerjee, 1962– —Childhood
and youth. 2. Bengali Americans—Biography.
3. Bengali Americans—Food. 4. Bengali
Americans—Social life and customs. 5. Cooking,
Indic. 6. Food habits—Kansas. 7. Food habits—
India—Bengal. 8. Kansas—Biography. I. Title.
E184.B26F87 2013
394.1'2095414—dc23   2013005215

Photo, page ii: The author's family when they first
moved to Kansas. Clockwise from top left: Sandeep
(brother), Sachin (father), Nina, and Sipra (mother).

For Anna and Nate

So this is how you swim inwards.
So this is how you flow outwards. So this is how you pray.

MARY OLIVER

Contents

Author's Note

Biting through the Skin: An Indian Kitchen in America's Heartland is a memoir that takes place primarily during what Virginia Woolf called "that great Cathedral space which was childhood." In this journey in food, I have privileged my memory over the memories of others.

Prologue

I am always combusting something.

I learned this from Joan Ruvinsky, a meditation teacher. If you throw wood into a fire, it burns; put food into your stomach, it does the same. For years, I did not notice that I was a version of larger elements. Blood runs through veins like rivers, through capillaries like lesser tributaries, some unseen under the skin, just as the earth's circulatory system trundles along into its vast, pooling heart, the ocean. The planet's fluidity mimics the watery element in my mouth that intimately creates taste. Sound itself reveals secrets and animates air. I stand in twilight, the wind blowing over the Missouri farm where my husband and I now live. Soft, turbulent, whispery and still by turns, the wind moans between trees down the drive, snaps near my ear as an owl skims past just out of sight, mimics breath. In and out, my earth expands and contracts with all the breathers everywhere: a rhythmic pulsing that vibrates the world.

I've heard meditators say you can hear that pulsing tone, and I routinely hear and break it by a stray thought about the dog's shots or the milk forgotten or whatever is the matter with Aunt T—, until that pulse disappears, spinning away into mist and hope.

And so, it seems to me, everything can be broken: into duplicity, into multiplicity. Science shows us molecules when we see whole people, neurons when there is blood, hydrogen particles in water. What, then, is irreducible, indivisible?

I add my personality to those of a group and watch as the relationships settle into a new pattern, changing the surface of things like ripples on a great body of water. I use a kitchen dropper and mete out almond extract, or vanilla, or orange into a recipe. If it drops into liquid, it transforms itself into the whole. Water to water. But a rock outside my door dropped onto the lawn stays separate. Our bodies are the same, separate, specious in life and assimilating to the great good earth at death, releasing our spirits at last to a nether place. Until then, all I have of indivisibility is secondhand knowledge.

In my search for an indivisible future that works, I keep spiraling back to a connection between myself, the earth, and India. Ancient cultures have never abandoned this interconnectedness and now, at midlife, it keeps rising up to meet me, something writer and activist for ecology and culture Helena Norberg-Hodge once noted. I began by thinking that growing up Indian in Kansas was mine alone. I now see that all families are small pockets of culture that hand their rituals, personalities and gifts, heritage and love down to the next generation through food rituals. Food holds memory. It holds story. It can represent who we are.

Usually, there are wider cultural events and habits that help shore up family traditions: Fourth of July celebrations mimic independence battles, and the food to celebrate (corn on the cob and fried chicken, perhaps) follows the farm cycle of pullets ready to become fryers and sweet corn planted in time to harvest and serve. Children in the Midwest learn that story early. For me, isolated in my pocket with no similar families nearby, food rituals became the only way my heritage was passed on. Northern Indian Bengali tradition came to me in Kansas via tomato chutney and *keema* curry, through the order in which spices were added to a dish and, indeed, which spices were selected. Northern India came to me through the use of whole grains for health stemming from Ayurvedic times: yogurt for digestion, vegetables combined in particular ways.

In the founding texts of Ayurvedic medicine, written down in the first century BCE, the treatises decree that the body needs to be kept in a state of equilibrium with its environment. We should, the *Caraka-Samhita* and *Susruta-Samhita* say, adjust our diets to seasonal variations in climate and produce, and six principal tastes divided into two groups: hot (pungent, acidic, salty) and cold (sweet, astringent, bitter). While the principles of Ayurvedic medicine shaped Indian cooking across its many regions, gradually the modern idea of mixing hot and cold foods in the same meal or dish to create a sublime blend of the six essential tastes emerged. I had no idea that Ayurvedic medicine was the culinary foundation of what my mother did in the kitchen until I was an adult: that long history and those layers of influence were not on my mind when she balanced salt with a little sugar in many dishes, or black pepper with cooling yogurt, or when she placed a chutney on the table that mixed both cloying sweetness with the sour bite of tamarind.

The system focused on the reaction of the body to the food after it entered the stomach—its postdigestive reaction, so to speak. It tied individual temperament and body type to particular foods. Food and its preparation were among the most important issues when choosing a diet to improve or maintain temperament and health.

The system relied heavily on individuals paying careful attention to their reactions to particular foods, something that might have been easier in the world of the Ayurvedic scholar. In that world, around 5000 BCE, there weren't quick-market cupcakes with a list of thirty or forty ingredients.

For years, I have been miserly in what I shared of my family's traditional Bengali foods. I kept the door firmly closed on the story of each dish: the story created by my family and the years of eating and preparing it in Kansas, and the older story from India, from the trees that fruited and the grains that ripened half a world away. The texture of a cooked grain of rice, firm yet a little pulpy on the fingertip, the slide of smooth mango down the throat: there are many portals to the heart.

If you are lucky, you see connections even in aromatic spices. Such tiny, brown bits of larger things are indeed Whitman's "journey-work of the stars." A recipe is the journey-work, the template, of culture and family, as well as tangible evidence of what we're willing to share of both. I read a recipe and see great expanses of land, cultivars of grain and vegetable, stunning lengths of history, and I imagine someone who feeds me, the dance behind the routine of cooking, the pop of memory, and the sizzle of love. Making that leap, trusting that the people of my home state of Kansas, and later Missouri, could see the gift presented with each meal, was a long time coming. Food was my tether to heritage; it revealed my world and transformed me into someone willing to share that story with others.

Something my daughter, Anna, once said comes to me now: "I find it fascinating how unaware I was when my mind was changing."

My first memories of trips to India while growing up were of my grandparents, a neighbor girl named Sweeti, and the craggy faces of rickshaw drivers. Behind these vivid mind pictures, though, was a feeling that loosens something under my sternum. It stemmed from the awe of seeing my father look taller, more vitally part of each meal, each conversation, like he returned to himself when we traveled there; of watching my mother settle into an old routine that I had never seen. Laughter was relaxed, conversation fluid. I felt an easing of a tightly held tension I did not know we had.

I am six and sitting alone on a black bus seat. My legs swing, almost kicking the back of the seat in front of me. The windows have a horizontal bar to slide them open or shut and there is a small wedge open at the top of mine. Ahead of me about five rows are the backs of the heads of my family: wispy hair, surprisingly gray for a fortyish father, flies about in streaks of sun slanting through the windows and reveals glimpses of a smooth, bald brown pate. This, the very top of my *baba*, is a head and shoulders above the tidy bun sitting quietly on my mother's neck, and stair-stepped down from her is just the tip of my wavy-haired brother's head. I lift my chin to watch as others leave the bus to buy papaya juice or a mango, or to stroll around the small highway pull-off until the driver is ready to continue on the switchback road up, up, and nauseatingly up through the blue Nilgiri Hills near Chennai. My stomach feels queasy from sickness, but I have been told to eat, hence my bully separateness from the rest of my family.

I have a banana in my lap, the small brown Indian kind full of flavor, and have just finished a sandwich my mother packed this morning. A crowd has gathered around the bus and far below me, I see a small child standing and looking straight into my eyes. He wears shorts and a buttoned shirt of some indeterminate color and he stands as tall as the elbows of the older children near him. No one else in the crowd looks at my window. His eyes stay steady though the crowd jostles him and the ragged hem of his shirt rucks up. I startle as I realize he has seen me eat the last bites of my bread. He has watched me swallow. I look at him more closely and see his hands are cupped.

I suddenly feel the bulkiness of the gummed bread still in my throat and stare at the banana in my lap. I want a drink but do not call out for one. My mother is talking earnestly, using her hands and tipping her head, making a point that causes my father to chuckle. *Do not waste your food, Nin,* she would admonish, and I look back to the boy and lift my banana to peel it. But I cannot do it. I feel the black vinyl seat stick to the backs of my thighs as I lift my torso up. Not high enough. I stand and the vinyl pulls free of my skin. I reach out the top of my window, toss the banana out, and watch as it drops and wobbles through the hot air. All else freezes as it makes its diver's arc, end over end. The sounds of vendors, of the driver's radio, of talking tourists, fade. The milling people themselves, in their colorful saris, with their turbans and beards pulled tight under the chin, blur. Then, just before the boy's outstretched hand can close around the fruit, the smell of the idling bus engine reaches my nose and I sit back quickly. My grandparents said just last night not to "encourage them," so I glance up to make sure no one saw.

Now, the bread in my throat goes down and I swallow audibly. I hope I will not be hungry later, and I look down once more at the boy. He has deftly caught the banana, though sometimes I imagine it dropping in the dirt first before he snatches it up. He takes quick bites straight through the bitter peel, as if someone might get to it still. I imagine what banana peel tastes like and what the soft, fleshy fruit would feel like beneath it on my tongue. I rub my tongue behind my front teeth and grimace. Then, I am frantic. What if my mother sees that the peel is not in my trash? Will she ask what became of the fruit? She walks back to check on me and never looks into the wilted paper sandwich wrapping. She pats my head and goes back to her seat as the bus pulls away.

I realize now how paralyzed I was seeing a child beg for food. I had seen beggars in India asking for money, but none had affected me as much as that boy. During our meals around a shellacked wooden table in Kansas, I spent inordinate amounts of time hiding foods that I didn't like. Peas were pushed under crusts of bread, and *korola*, a gourd that my father and I called "blood purifier" to indicate its bitterness, I mashed with my fork to subdue. After the parts I didn't like were sorted to satisfaction, I ate the comfort foods, like potatoes with black pepper, or rice with minced meat, with such relish that I would finish in five minutes the meal my mother wanted us to linger over. Every dinnertime, at exactly 5:30, my father would turn on the national news with Huntley and Brinkley. All conversation stopped so he could hear. My back was to the television so I had nothing to do but stare at the foods my mother had prepared and rest my head on my hand.

The cautionary stories of starving children in India bandied about in Kansas to force kids to finish their peas did not apply to my life until that moment on the bus. Now I understand I had formed an acute sense of privilege in being born who and what and where I was. My family lived with this dichotomy all their lives, but that's when I saw it first. My grandfather felt that the economy ran by families hiring a cook, a driver, a gardener. They kept order by separating people into groups that served and supervised. In many ways, I think that moment on the bus was the impetus behind my later development work in the Peace Corps, behind my teenage squabbles with my family over politics after I began turning around and watching the news unfold each night on TV. In the end, for me, there was that boy, eating a fruit with absolute concentration and no quibbling, peel and all.

Biting through the Skin

Transformation

There is something to be done at this season. Something to be done. I tap my pencil on the island counter and look outside my kitchen window at rolling Missouri farmland, brittle-brown and orange as it always is at this time of year. The festival of Bijoya Dashami means good wishes need to be passed on to family elders and friends; I know it. But because this festival day occurs on the tenth day after the first new moon of autumn, a day highlighted on the cycle of the Bengali calendar but not on mine with the cute photos of dogs, the dates change within the season each year. I am never quite sure when the calls to the elders should be made, and there is no one to remind me here in the county of Howard, in the state of Missouri, in the United States.

In the Indian state of Bengal, my family's homeland, Durga Puja marks days of celebration when the goddess Durga, deliverer of dangers including those of selfishness, jealousy, prejudice, hatred, anger, and ego, visits each year, and the day she departs, Bijoya Dashami, is for inclusion, for eating well with others, for the blowing of conch shells and the scent of food. Each autumn, when the weighted air of the summer monsoon rains lifts, three separate goddess festivals occur: Durga first, then Lakshmi, goddess of wealth and prosperity, feminine beauty and grace, and then Kali, fearsome destroyer. These three *pujas* are celebrated by various food-related activities: for Durga,

Bengalis start by fasting one day, eating simple vegetarian dishes like tasty and comforting *aloo dam* and *luchi* the second day, and then switching to succulent meat curries on the third day. Day four is the day for sweets to be given and received, among them my favorite *sandesh* and the seemingly fancier *rosogolla*, bobbing in syrup. Elders are offered *pronam*, or respects, men give each other three hugs—right side, left side, then right again—and children receive blessings. Hopeful thoughts turn to peace and prosperity. On the final night, the carefully crafted figures of Durga, sometimes made of clay, sometimes of wood or other materials, almost always painted and dressed artistically, which have been set about on *pandals* during the puja, are sent on their way in the rite of *bhashan* by being immersed in nearby waterways. The community reconnects with friends and loved ones in public and expansive celebration. It is the perfect time for it: the autumn in Bengal is for rejoicing. The monsoon is finished, the hills become a mixture of gold and green, and rice ripens in the fields ready for harvest.

But mine is an American tale.

It was impossible for my parents, with such joyful and poignant memories, to re-create these times in America's heartland. And so it was small details that were weighty in Kansas, where I grew up. My mother fussed about correctly preparing the foods, how many dishes would be served, what clothes I would wear. There were no grand celebrations to attend that would have tempered this focus and made it preliminary and ultimately unimportant to the event. Holy festivals were done behind closed doors in my childhood; they were private affairs where our attic fan blew away cooking aromas before guests arrived. Perhaps because I had never seen an autumn in India or felt the air lift and lighten after the monsoon season, the idea of rejoicing didn't occur to me.

This autumn another festival season comes in serial celebrations: days of celebrating Durga, then Lakshmi at the autumn full moon, then Kali fourteen days later on the new moon, one after another. The pujas bring another chance for me to connect to this vast and rich history of my family. I mark my calendar on the days that the Indian Association in a nearby larger town is hosting events in honor of the goddesses. Then I note that a service club I belong to is having its annual ham and bean dinner to raise funds for scholarships on one of the puja days. I am really needed as a dishwasher. Not to worry, there are two other Indian events. But an interview for *Savor Missouri*, a regional food and wine book I am completing, simply must be on one of those other days, and the interview is in a town four hours away, necessitating an overnight stay. Durga, deliverer of dangers, and Lakshmi, goddess of wealth and prosperity, feminine beauty and grace, are yet again set aside. Fearsome Kali, whom you really don't want to rouse, frowns.

Dishwashing duties in the kitchen of Fayette Middle School supercede Durga? Kali, for goodness' sake? Generations of my Bengali family, of Mukerjees, of Banerjis, and others, in a long, friendly grouping smile sadly and quizzically at me from Indian antiquity. *That's it?* I picture them saying. And I swear I see my maternal great-grandmother, Renuka, cross her arms and tap her foot. And the old man just over there, Rup Chand, my father's grandfather, lifts his palms up in amazement and then sits down heavily, shaking his head.

It gets worse. The day of the festival, I stand on a rubber mat in the cafeteria kitchen of Fayette Middle School and I realize not one person in this group of friends knows I am missing such an important Indian event. When I turn quickly in my tennis shoes, a sharp squeaking emanates across the kitchen, but the twenty or so other women hard at work stirring beans or making corn bread do not notice. My wet rubber gloves are yellow, and the stainless steel spray nozzle runs amok only occasionally when I fumble. My denim apron has damp splotches where the superheated water bounced off a bowl and caught me in the stomach. If I had been at the puja, I would have been in a sari, probably my pale celery-green silk with the delicate ivory border embroidered with gold, and my feet would have been bare. The silk would have flowed around my legs and made a rustling noise as I sat cross-legged in the temple hall. I have known these ham and bean ladies seventeen years, yet I have kept India, and a good half of who I am, a secret.

Inside my small pocket of culture, I squelch water beneath my feet in a middle school kitchen while yearning to visit a temple. It has taken my lifetime to reach this impasse.

In the 1960s, my hometown of Pittsburg, Kansas, rich in its own story of assimilation, had no particular interest in differences. There I was playing softball, riding my ten-speed, and going to the Dairy Queen, eyes bright, fingers sticky, all the while losing my identity. Securely hidden behind our front door, however, India could be found in the aroma in the air, the taste of cardamom, the brush of my mother's silk sari, and the cadence of my father's speech. In pre–long-grain rice America, eating was cause for inquiry, and so we kept our traditional foods private. If a friend came over, soda and chips were provided. If a meal was called for, then burgers it was. My lunch at school may have consisted of peanut butter and jelly or grilled cheese or tuna, just like Beth's or LuAnn's or Kathy's, but not dinner, and it was during five o'clock meals around a shellacked wooden table in Kansas that I found passion.

India held court around Mom's table. The impact of warm spice aromas, the taste of bitter gourd and cooling yogurt, signaled a cultural boundary I could cross even with my American upbringing. Flavor and taste were my inheritance. Though I lost the dress, the ease of language, and the rituals of India, the foods of the subcontinent were ever there. Simple cauliflower and potato *bhaji*; thin *jhol* curries, redolent of cinnamon, cardamom, and cloves, eaten with a bit of aromatic rice; warm *luchis* rolled up around a little sugar, all so satisfying. Like many American immigrants, I held my home culture close to the vest, near the heart. I did not share well then. Not sharing was a recipe for sorting people who did or did not want to know; a recipe for private versus public foods; for a vastly different world outside our front door. In many ways, my family wanted to be ordinary in Kansas, yet maintaining our heritage meant we were not even close. Half my world became secret. Necessitating this secrecy was a grand move.

In the early days of a 1964 Chicago summer, a small moment occurred. My family, surrounded by boxes and bags packed with all manner of possessions, trundled themselves off to Kansas from the Windy City, the second such move in a year. I don't know if there were kitchen utensils involved, nor am I sure of particular furnishings that were carted into the trailer, but within the clothing boxes saris were carefully folded so as not to form odd creases, probably with the silks separated from the cottons. I feel certain that two red children's coats with pointy hoods trimmed in white fluff were pressed down into cardboard by my mother, and I know that a sled emerged Kansas-side, so it must have made the cut.

After wending through Illinois, my father merged onto I-69 South in Kansas. My parents did not snack in the car, that New World lack of respect for expensive cars not imaginable to them. They stopped, as they almost always did in later years, at the Pleasanton hamburger joint north of town near the railroad tracks for chocolate-vanilla ice-cream twists. A full hour and a half south of Kansas City, they came upon the valley of Fort Scott. The land, flat for miles, dipped slightly and broadly there, visible only with a squint and a tilt of the head, and there was a surprising amount of vegetation, deciduous and leafy, along fencerows and in woody copses.

It was a long drive and they may not have seen the valley. My mother, busy comforting my brother, Sandeep, and me, and my father, preoccupied by the two-lane road, would not have noticed anything dramatic. The valley became more perceptible to us over time as we lived in southeast Kansas, especially after a tornado season or two when twisters were noted for sailing over low spots in the land.

Whatever they saw is specifically lost to those moments in the car. They were six months fresh from India. Chicago, their first home in the United States, had proven too cold, too large and impersonal, though full of pockets of Indian immigrants around the city: groups that socialized, raised children with common ideals, and conducted religious festivals together. They traded that comfort for a small Kansas town with almost no American minorities and absolutely no other Indians until years later. My mother was twenty-two and my father thirty-five. As we came into Pittsburg, Kansas, a town of twenty thousand people nearly a thousand miles south and west of the better-known Pittsburgh in Pennsylvania, there was a cemetery neatly plotted on the right.

India was at war with China along its Himalayan border when my parents left Asia in 1963. More of India's resources were poured into defense. My father felt stifled there, like there were barriers to rising professionals, not support. He watched men in his village ride their bicycles to work, ties flapping against white button-up shirts. A bike seemed a paltry reward for hard work to a young man who had heard about the Chevrolets, Fords, Plymouths, and Buicks in the United States. More could be achieved —television and word of mouth told him so.

My parents arrived in North America to find agitation here, too. The United States was facing rising troubles in Vietnam, and Martin Luther King had delivered his "I Have a Dream" speech in response to civil rights issues in August. The US postal service had issued zip codes for the first time to implement some order, lava lamps and touch-tone phones had been launched, and a loaf of bread was twenty-two cents. When my parents purchased a television, a cheery Dick Van Dyke was on weekly. Just thirty days after arriving in Chicago, Mom walked into the lobby of the hotel where my parents stayed before finding their first home on US soil and noticed a gathering crowd. The Chicago passersby and hotel workers jostled for a view around a television set as the news broke: Kennedy shot in Dallas, November 22. Eyes wide, Mom breathed slowly and watched the crowd react—stunned disbelief and worry.

My parents cared about these things. Their lives, encased in the little car headed south toward southeast Kansas a few months later, echoed on another scale the seismic changes of country. My father's father was an accountant in Hazaribagh, a small town (even with a population of over one hundred thousand people, fourteen tigers, twenty-five panthers, and four hundred sambar deer in residence in the nearby national park, it did not get "city" status in India) in what is now the state of Jharkhand, India, and came from generations of Mukerjees there. My mother came from the Banerji line, most recently of Ranchi, a larger town a couple of hours away over rough roads. My parents came from good families and inherited status, and they left all that behind for the promise of a life built on what they did with their own hands—a bigger world than what India offered in the early 1960s. My dad was one of many Indian men who left the country that decade in droves, the Asian brain drain. There was no urgency in their lives, no knifepoint of decision other than that of youth, pressing intelligence, and drive. The foods, family connections, and familiar ease of their own cultural and spiritual life trailed my parents like diminishing waves, and they may not have known for years what was in their wake. They had a vested interest now in this new land and in the belief that they had made the right choice.

Perhaps it was disconcerting for my parents to hear the bickering of politicians and the unhappiness of a culture in flux when they had just given up so much to come to the United States, but I think it also energized them. Here they could participate, have opinions, weigh in. The same could be said in India, but this was the New World. The old one was stagnant. My father watched the nightly news at 5:30 P.M. with the express purpose of having an opinion to discuss with his coworkers at McNally Engineering Company the next day. Being informed equaled nationhood.

But nothing in my life of play and preschool passed judgment. I was simply there, coming back to myself again and again. The food of India was my tether to heritage. My mother kneaded whole wheat flat bread, roti, on our kitchen counter and mixed rice with yogurt for my breakfast. Flour dusted her hands as she pulled the dough into small balls from the larger lump, as she palmed those balls into smoothness before using the rolling pin to make the required thin rounds, ready for the hot, flat cast-iron pan on the stove. Lunch was often dal and a vegetable. She mashed the simple meals and I pumped my chubby fists and swallowed. She dusted her fingers free of wheat flour into cotton kitchen towels, gathered her fingers to her thumb and helped me. And since I carried my world with me, my surroundings had no influence except to offer up an alphabet block or a blue ball. To offer up a familiar texture of ceiling as I went down for a nap. There was no comfort or theology outside myself. If I was surprised to find myself in the basement of a southeast Kansas preschool at Pittsburg State College, it was by the capriciousness of the outside human world, not my own within.

Long before I began reclaiming the food story of my grandmothers, I bent forward, fingertips outstretched, and snared a Tootsie Roll off the asphalt at the Pittsburg, Kansas, homecoming parade. Because I was young, not yet three feet tall, I was at the front of the parade crowd. Rising up from the candy grab, I could see the 4-H club and their horses coming. The wind flipped the brims of the riders' cowboy hats, the girls raising their hands to keep them in place, the boys just tipping down their chins. The glistening coats of the horses rippled in the sun. Their legs looked enormous and their hooves made hollow clopping noises on the pavement, muffled once the Pittsburg High School Marching Dragons started up behind them. Eyeing the horses, the pom-pom girls holding the band banner marched in place trying to create a larger gap. A little backwash of clarinets and flutes crowded the trombones and trumpets. The drummers in the back rows started to step higher. The precision of the lines warped until the director walking alongside signaled the row leaders. It could have been a pileup with a less skilled band.

In front of me, Shriner clowns in tall hats maneuvered their big-wheel tricycles so that by turning the handles hard, they kept from grazing toes at the edge of the parade. They lifted their knees, covered in ballooning yellow fabric, almost to their chins before pushing downward to the rhythm of squeaking pedals. Other children darted out, quick and sure, and nabbed wrapped candy thrown on the pavement. My father would later become a Shriner, and though he never rode the asphalt on a trike, he did many things to raise funds for Shriner burn hospitals around the country. He emerged from Harzaribagh in Bihar, India, the son of Dwijen Nath Mukerjee, an accountant for the government of Kashmir and for the military in World War I, and Indu Banerji of Kolkata, to mix with Shriners in Kansas. Years later, my mother would rise in the ladies auxiliary of the Shrine, Daughters of the Nile, to be Queen of the Nile. For her crowning event, she had all the ladies wear Indian saris instead of evening gowns. She had me and my teenage friends model Indian *selwar kamis* in a runway walk on a stage that same evening. India emerged that night but many might have mistaken it for a variation on the Shriner use of symbols of Eastern desert kingdoms. It was thrilling and mysterious and all wrapped up in the clothing of one evening event. Mostly, though, unlike many immigrants in American cities who socialized mainly with others also displaced from homelands a world away, my parents made a conscious effort to be in *this* land. They tackled moving to a small Kansas town with verve and a sense of adventure.

My father had met Ed McNally in India when Ed was checking on the Indian branch of his Kansas engineering firm and foundry. McNally's company did coal systems engineering and plant design. By family account, Ed offered my father a spot in Kansas if he should ever be interested in living in a small town in the United States. At the time, Baba worked for a large international engineering firm based in Chicago. After one winter in Chicago, though, used to warmer climes as well as a dense and enveloping community of people involved in their lives, my parents chose to move.

Today, I see this as Kansas beauty: the politeness, the nod to sorrow, the idea that you should be watching where you're going. I am comfortable being around midwesterners. In an airport once, a line was waiting to board a charter plane to Mexico. To me these businessmen and women, farmers, and teachers waiting in the Kansas City airport looked at ease if a little rumpled. They were not clad in black like the New Yorkers nearby, nor were they bright and shiny like coastal tourists. A lady in line turned and her lavender raincoat revealed a light rose-colored floral dress sticking to thick calves encased in hose a shade too dark. She looked like any number of the women lining the parade route each year in my hometown. I felt I could approach that woman if I needed to, ask her anything. Kansans populate my personal heartland.

I wonder if my great-grandmother, or even my grandmother, could have predicted Pittsburg, a place without designation or limit, distant from northern India. Could they have foretold my Big Smith overalls and hiking boot childhood? The white rubber caps we wore to swim at the YMCA? The Pla-Mor

Roller Rink with the weld-wire fence sides that allowed parents to watch the revolving skaters while sitting in their cars parked alongside?

My relatives could never have known about the big-leaved catalpa trees or the mimosas with their frothy pink blooms growing along neighborhood streets near Lakeside Junior High. I squished over partly decomposed fallen flowers each year with the wheels of my Schwinn bike. Always, some tendrils of bloom adhered to the black asphalt while others waved in the air. Later, when I was thirteen, I rolled over them on my orange ten-speed with the curled-over handlebars. Each year, the mimosas looked more exotic than the oaks, cottonwoods, and elms around them. In them, I now see a link to the Indian flowering canopy of trees—the jacaranda, champac, bottlebrush, floss silk, and more. Each year in Kansas, I rolled over my right of *knowing* that beauty, oblivious and drunk on youth and Slurpees.

The physical layout of Pittsburg is a far cry from the India of my grand-mother, too. My grandparents' hill city in India rests on high, flat plains, and acres and acres of rice paddies can be seen from rock outcroppings like Tagore Hill near their house. Fields squared into patches of rice stretch out indefinitely into hazy sunsets. Southeastern Kansas, scarred from open-strip pit mines for coal and other minerals until rehabilitation projects planted trees, is unnaturally crumpled into crowded hillocks and small ponds in places, the result of earth pushed up and piled for the "Pits." My friends and I would go to the Pits for swimming or for parties. I was always leery of the aqua color of the rehabilitated water, though, so clear in the strong Kansas sunlight that you could see that neither fish nor plant life existed in its depths.

Small Kansas towns are somewhat predictable. The main street and cross-roads in Pittsburg are grid-like, the intersections and architecture squared off, and while there are many parked cars, few people walk about on the swept sidewalks. There is a park on the fringe of town. There are churches on many corners.

In contrast, Indian cities are chaotic. Roads come slashing into intersections from many angles, pedestrians crowd traffic, doorways curve into arches, vendors and rickshaws vibrate with humanity. Ancient temples encased in centuries-old blackened stone peek out from behind newer buildings and movie billboards. Holy men with ashes smeared on their foreheads mumble the 108 holy names for God and amble through crowds of shoppers. Cars seem to lurch down the byways avoiding people, carts, and cows standing majestically in their path. From a distance, without the sounds, the motion of an Indian motorway is like a river, flowing forcefully in the path of least resistance.

In Kansas, there were no masses of humanity pressing inward on the driving lanes. Crosswalks were adhered to, generally. However, Pittsburg *was* the kind of town in which people pulled over to the side of the road for funeral processions. Cars pulled over when they saw the lead car with its headlights on, even on the highway. Sometimes, you could be in a car gunning fifty-five or sixty and brake to a dead stop. Highway 69 North outside of town led past a large graveyard with many empty plots, so you had to watch out. I remember Mom looking frantically into the rearview mirror to make sure the car behind us had seen the headlights. You never knew what was coming.

Otherwise the main characteristic of Pittsburg traffic was most noticeable at four-way stop signs. People tended to take their time at four-ways, communication slow and easy as they looked left, making eye contact with the driver there to make sure he didn't feel it was his turn, then glancing right to do the same thing. This language of the four-way stop continued until a car was urged on with a finger wave—no, no, go on, you first.

The public spectacle of India garnered wide-eyed wonder from visitors, but Kansas provoked a bored glance through tinted car windows along Interstate 70. The 423-mile stretch of Kansas interstate between Colorado and Missouri was in mere drive-by status for most Americans. Few inside the thousands of cars, SUVs, and trucks that cruised along marked the moment when, with a spreading flush, the fields greened in the spring. Even the wind was ignored by passersby. Still, it blew its image over the grasses, pushing stalks down in masses as big as several city blocks to release with a flourish all at once. This recompense of Kansas beauty came from staying put, not passing through.

India, too, has suffered from bad publicity. People in 1960s Kansas were admonished to clean their plates because of India's starving children. The beauty of its landscape, rich food traditions, and deep history were not part of the story.

Food rituals connected my disparate world. My mother's refrigerator had the makings for egg curry and vegetable *tarkari*. If I peeked into her cabinets, I'd find chickpea flour and whole wheat flour for roti separated by a shelf from all-purpose white. The outside world held the tastes of melt-in-your-mouth grilled cheese sandwiches on white bread from the PX, a small sandwich grill and candy shop, that we ate at lunchtime sitting on the curb by Lakeside

Junior High, our elbows bumping. The buttery sandwiches were pressed flat and left crumbs to lick off the corners of our lips. PICCO (Pittsburg Ice Cream Company) ice cream, plain vanilla or black cherry, was a hands-down favorite, as was Daylight Donuts on Sundays. I would inevitably pick a white cake doughnut with coconut icing, my dad a bear claw, my brother a glazed or a long john, and Mom usually a cinnamon roll. We got twenty-five-cent hamburgers with crunchy dill pickle slices at Griff's on Tenth and Broadway, where my friend Beth worked for a time. We wiped our chins with paper napkins to catch the dribbles from the burgers, which were as large as a man's hand, at 1106 S. Broadway and called them 1106 Grease Burgers as a compliment.

If I had to pick a taste that brings back Pittsburg to me, though, it would be fried chicken. Two restaurants sprang up early in Crawford County history—Chicken Annie's and Chicken Mary's—to serve crispy and delicious fried food with slaw, vinegary potato salad, and spaghetti, reflecting the Italian and Germanic-Baltic heritage of the area; local history on the plate. Even today, the restaurants, sitting three hundred yards from each other, inspire fierce debates over who has the best chicken.

For me, there did not seem to be a bridge between the foods and landscape of Kansas and India. There were never cumin-spiced vegetables next to fried chicken on dinner plates, for instance, or lamb burgers on the fast-food menu. Plus, unlike anyone I knew in Pittsburg, my mother made cheese. In Old World Pittsburg, this was quite usual, as it is in India, but not so in the Pittsburg of the 1960s.

Chhana, homemade cheese, is good for savory dishes, but Mom made it for Bengali sweets. My childhood favorite, *sandesh*, is a northern Indian specialty. I lived for when she would make this for us. It never occurred to me that my friends would be interested; they were part of my Kansas life. I did not give them a chance to taste the heartfelt flavors of Mom's handiwork and thereby cut myself off from shared joy. These days, I knead lumps of the cheese on the counter like my mother before me. My elbows jut out and the heels of my hands ache a little from the downward pressure on the softening white ball. Cheese-like, it waits.

To make sandesh, take one gallon of milk and bring it to a boil; squeeze in the juice of a lemon and watch the milk curdle and separate into floating hunks (curd) among the whey (liquid); listen to your children say "eewwww" as they watch over your shoulder. Strain it and wrap it in cheesecloth that you tie around the kitchen faucet to drip-dry overnight like my mother did. Or tie the cheesecloth ends around a wooden spoon, hang your new bag over the pot, and slide the whole thing into the refrigerator. At this point, I usually have a moment of panic when I can't find the fabric I always use for cheesecloth: a bit of an old faded cotton sari of my mother's, orange with gray-green flowers. When I find the piece of fabric, I notice again that the cotton is loosely woven, and I remember that its twin, another bit taken from the same six-foot length of cloth, was used to tie up cheese in my mother's kitchen in the 1960s. After six to eight hours of drying time, remove the dried chhana from your own special cloth and knead, or do as Mom does nowadays and put one cup of chhana at a time in a food processor and spin for three minutes. Put the mass into a heavy pan and heat, add one cup of sugar and a bit of dried milk, orange zest, or vanilla, and cook until it is the correct texture—smooth, a little dry, so that it sticks to the top of your mouth when you taste it, not crumbly. Form into warm ovals about one by one and a half inches and press with your thumb. Or press into special, decorative sandesh molds, if you have them. Cool to room temperature. Eat.

There is a trick to getting it right, though. Transforming the milk into sandesh seems simple, and it is easy to make the cheese, but then things can go awry. Just the right amount of kneading (or food processing) makes the cheese softly stick a bit between forefinger and thumb. I am forever making this dish in such a way that even though it tastes right, it lacks the correct texture and becomes so dry it forms tiny crunchy balls. My mother had various explanations for this and the one I treasure the most is that the milk must not have been fresh enough. She bought her milk at a grocery, too, and it made a perfect batch.

In a recipe, you add this and this and this and you get a wholly new, perfectly textured creation with unique flavor that carries with it images of the past. In all probability it looks and tastes as if it just popped out of Grandma's oven, no matter that forty years have passed, that five or more US presidents have governed, and a woman has ruled India. Step-by-step memories. It is not as easy to shape a life that includes all the important bits from the past as it is to follow a recipe, especially when you leave your homeland. I asked my mother to *please* estimate the quantity of spices I needed to use for one of her dishes. I told her that "put in some ginger" wasn't specific enough. She cupped her palm and showed me the size of the well: *that* much ginger.

As we stood with our heads tipped together, I tried to translate that cupped palm to my stainless steel measuring spoons, to balance that cavity of space against the scent and taste of the finished dish, against the aroma of steaming basmati rice, roasting cumin seeds, and cinnamon sticks in hot oil. Then I shrugged, and guessed.

And a new food narrative began.

CHHANA (SIMPLE CHEESE)

Makes about 2 cups

1 gallon whole milk, as fresh as possible
½–¾ cup lemon juice
cheesecloth

In a heavy stockpot, bring the milk to a full boil, and when it starts to rise in the pot, add the lemon juice a little at a time until the milk separates. Strain the curd from the remaining liquid (whey) and place into the cheesecloth. Squeeze out as much water as possible with your hands (be careful as the liquid will be hot). Hang the cheesecloth around the kitchen faucet or tie it to a wooden spoon placed over a pot and slide it into the refrigerator for 6 to 8 hours.

To make plain cheese or cubes for savory dishes: After placing the cheese curds into the cheesecloth, squeeze out as much water as possible and place the cheesecloth and its contents on a clean counter. Fill the stockpot with water to make it heavy and place it on top of the cheesecloth overnight. In the morning, cut the dried chhana into cubes. Serve as plain cheese. Or, heat a tablespoon of vegetable oil in a saucepan. When hot, place one layer of cubes in and fry until slightly brown, turn, and repeat until all pieces are golden. Wonderful plain or lightly fried in vegetable curries like *chhanar dalna* [page 150], or in *chhanar payesh* [page 160].

SANDESH (SWEET BENGALI CONFECTION)

Makes about 24 pieces

chhana from one gallon whole milk, dried for 6–8 hours in cheesecloth
   (see recipe above)
1 cup sugar
¼ cup dried milk
1 teaspoon vanilla (optional)

1 tablespoon flour, if using sandesh molds

Take the lump of dried chhana from its cheesecloth and spin in a food processor until smooth and a little tacky to the touch, about 5 minutes. If you have strong arms and time, knead the chhana on a hard surface until you reach the same texture. Test the texture between your forefinger and thumb. In a large well-seasoned iron or nonstick skillet, heat the chhana over medium heat. Add sugar, mix well. The mass will become moist; add dried milk and continue to stir over medium heat until it dries. If you plan to use sandesh molds, add flour and mix thoroughly. Once the sugar and dried milk are absorbed into the chhana, remove the pan from the heat, add vanilla if desired, and let cool a little. Form ovals about 1½ x 1 inch, or press sandesh into shaped molds of about the same size, and let cool. Sandesh can be kept at room temperature for one day and is best served fresh. Refrigerate after that point in an airtight container.

2

Two Brides

My part of the Mukerjee-Banerji narrative begins with spices. Women have always wielded ginger in my family: ginger as well as many other tiny pieces of larger things. I was too young to ask which spices my mother used in Kansas and my grandmother used during my first trips to India, but my nose selected what it needed. When you get down to it, what tied food traditions across centuries of births and deaths, two continents, and three primary languages in my family were aromatic bits and pieces.

This was true across India. Just as Pittsburg's popular fried chicken restaurants serve spaghetti as well as German potato salad as standard side dishes—disparate heritages together on the plate—an Indian kitchen reveals culture in its traditions.

Historically, there was no tight connection among the people of the Indus; all were from princely states with their own foods, customs, and calendars. If there was a common denominator in their recipes, it was the imaginative use of spices, with each one bringing a special flourish to a dish. It was this medley of tastes that perked up plainer dishes and gave Indian food its unique character.

India is more than a million square miles divided into thirty-one states and territories—not as big as the United States, but nothing to sneeze at geographically speaking. Terrain, local produce, history, and religion all play a role in the amazing variety of foods in India. The few dishes Westerners are used to seeing in Indian restaurants skim the surface of the food offered in one region. Some say Hindu Punjabis forced back across the border at the time of Pakistan's partition from India started the first restaurants in India in 1945. Their beehive-shaped tandoori ovens, which heat to 1,000°F, cooked bread, meat, and fish with astonishing speed, and they remain the perfect technology, even today, for this feat. Now, a mix of Punjabi and Mughal cuisine has become standard restaurant fare both in India and abroad.

Mughal descendants of Barber, who conquered India in 1526 and founded an Islamic empire that lasted until 1857, produced strong Persian influences in the food of certain regions in the north, my Bengali food included. The distinctive use of fresh and dried fruit, cashews, pistachios, and almonds in meat dishes as well as the use of a great many dairy products marked this cuisine. In my family recipes, this influence shows up in the dried raisin Mom inserted into each savory minced meat chop, the almonds in chicken biryani, the pistachios garnishing milk-based Bengali sweets. Another mark of Mughlai foods was the use of as many as twelve spices in a single dish, including the most expensive of them—saffron, cardamom, cinnamon, and cloves, all common spices in my mother's kitchen, with the exception of saffron, which was harder to come by in Kansas.

History was also clearly revealed in the food of Goa on the southwestern coast, an area held by the Portuguese in the past. Goans eat pork and duck, meats rarely seen in India outside the area, and introduced the use of the chili pepper to India. (So if you don't like the heat in some Indian foods, you are actually traditional—preferring flavorful but not hot dishes.) Goans also use vinegar, another Portuguese legacy, not tamarind, as is common in other areas of India, as a souring agent in dishes like vindaloo and for their chutneys.

The anglicized word *curry* might stem from *kari*, a South Indian word for "sauce," or from *tarkari*, a North Indian dish—but that is most likely happenstance. Clearly the sahibs and memsahibs loved the flavors of India. When they returned to England, they had their cooks grind up a mix of spices to sprinkle on staid fare. The world now knows this as "curry powder," and whatever is cooked with it is curry, not to be confused with curry leaves, which are sometimes used as flavoring, usually in whole form, in some Indian recipes.

But a whole gamut of spices is needed to produce the banquet of foods in India, and the women of my family knew it: asafetida powder, cumin, coriander, cardamom, cinnamon, cloves, mustard seeds, fenugreek, black pepper, ginger, saffron, nutmeg, turmeric, bay, and more. In cooking, they sometimes left the spices whole and sizzled them in hot oil, sometimes they roasted them, and at other times they ground and mixed them to make a paste with water. Each technique brought out a completely different aromatic flavor from the same spice. And they also used tamarind, coconuts and their milk, pistachios, cashews, and almonds. It can hit you when you step off an international flight in Delhi at the then usual arrival time of 2:00 A.M.: those scents oppressed by heat and mixed with tarmac and something earthy. Once, I opened a box of henna from a health food store in Missouri and the aroma struck me before I could focus on the words on the back of the box. Mumbai henna: my grandparents, the Delhi airport, jet lag, India.

In Bengal, family and friends connected over aromatic bits of cinnamon, cardamom, cloves, dried red chili, and more: in savory vegetarian or meat curries, in samosas and chops, in chutney recipes. But whole spices were not easy to conjure in Kansas—where bulk cinnamon sticks were more easily found in Woolworth's craft aisle than in the grocery store. In Kansas, ginger was purchased dried and powdered, as were cumin, coriander, and cayenne; whole spices like cardamom, cloves, dried red chilies, bay, and cinnamon sticks were purchased from Eastern groceries in Chicago, twelve hours away by car, during trips there or by friends who brought the spices to us. In other grand family moves, these spices had not been so rare.

When my grandmother made her bridal trip to her husband's family in 1925, finding spices was not an issue. She traveled from Rawalpindi in what is now Pakistan to Kolkata, a distance of around twelve hundred miles. My grandmother, my *didu*, was thirteen and newly married. The families would have known of each other, no doubt, through the complex and astonishing network of mothers, aunts, and cousins.

Her father would have studied the matter of her marriage to determine that my grandfather was a good match. The boy was of a good family, was old enough to have a profession, and could support her. As was typical of the era, she was not consulted, nor did she meet her future husband prior to the wedding. In keeping with the Indian penchant for all things astrological, the boy's birth chart was studied closely, as was my grandmother's. The premise: everything is linked and a predestined cosmic design is at play. The charts of my grandmother, Pratibha, and Amiya Banerji were congenial. This was more critical than a face-to-face meeting, which my ancestors knew could have spelled disaster—something ephemeral such as looks or personality could have gotten in the way.

There was a traditional celebration and ceremony that lasted for days. The women spent a day applying henna to my grandmother's hands and feet in designs ancient and swirling. There was the "first visit" by the bride's family, and the "first welcome" by the groom's. The families approached each other, procession-like, with gifts and sweets while conch shells were blown. Then my grandmother was brought in by her brothers, her head covered by the decorative border of her sari, her tinted feet and decorated hands showing, and my grandfather and she ceremonially made eye contact for the first time under white fabric held over their heads. They exchanged fragrant garlands of white and red flowers and later made seven circles around a sacred fire as they committed their vows. The young couple sat in their wedding finery (she in a red silk sari embellished with gold medallions, he in a white kurta with a conical white hat) while a priest recited Sanskrit verses. Rich biryanis, spicy dals, and lush sweets with strong milky tea were eaten throughout the bountiful days of marriage.

Then my grandmother traveled the long distance to Kolkata across varying terrain, mostly by train, carrying her customs and trousseau—several lovely saris, some embellished leather *chappals* for her feet, a *teep* box for the powder that she used to place the colorful dot on her forehead, and gold bangles on her arms. India, a country that has always done pomp well, was unsurpassed under the British Raj and in 1925, Rani, as my grandmother was called in the family, was dressed finely, surrounded and padded and bundled across the land.

Rani was Bengali but was raised Punjabi in her ways and manners. Her favorite foods and dress were that of a *patani*—someone from the north. Her Punjabi roots would have made many of the Indian recipes known in the West common to her: naan bread, *pakoras* (vegetable fritters), *saag paneer* (spinach with cheese).

Perhaps because she was just thirteen when she joined her new husband's household in Bengal, she quickly soaked up the kitchen customs—the Bengali ways fish should be prepared, the correct way to chop vegetables. Rani became the woman I knew as *Didu* in the bosom of the Banerji household, not her own. She helped in the kitchen where, as often as not, her mother-in-law cooked the meals. When her father-in-law had enough money, the extended family hired a *thakur*, a Bengali word meaning "image of god," a man who came to their home each morning to work in the kitchen, freshly bathed and wearing a clean dhoti.

In that household of five brothers and a mother and father, my grandmother was the only girl. Gradually, the other wives came along and my grandmother became the "eldest" daughter-in-law and held sway. She was young and mischievous. Family tales tell of her throwing a ball down the three stories of their multilevel home and when my grandfather would retrieve it, she would throw it again. I imagine her doing this with a giggle. I think it was a peculiar trait she had, to laugh indulgently even in the midst of talking. In all the later visits we made to India while I was growing up, I remember her words forming this way, the warm sound defusing almost any situation. When tea was delayed, a visit postponed, or the car not properly attended to, she chuckled. Most especially, when my grandfather was abrupt or even alarming in his reactions to these same circumstances, she chuckled. Didu made me feel that all the little annoyances of life were amusing.

After my grandfather was established in his work as a government administrator, he took his young bride off to start their independent life. They moved about India as the government took him first to the northern hills, next to the south, and they acquired another cook, Bhagwan Singh. *Bhagwan*, another word in India for God, or a godly person elevated in society, would cook a European breakfast for my mother and her three brothers: an egg, toast, porridge, and Ovaltine or chocolate. Family lore has it that my mother would wait until the last possible minute to eat her egg, often swallowing large chunks to get it over with, her large eyes tearing. No whole wheat roti and potatoes for Mom. Bhagwan Singh traveled with the family through the various postings, but when the call was to the far south, he declined. He was from the Himalayas and somehow could not make the adjustment. But for those early ten years or so of my mother's young life, he was the cook, and my grandmother left the breakfast choices more or less up to him. *Jai bhagwan* (Go with peace/love/God).

The next grand move for my family crossed the Bay of Bengal: my mother, eighteen in 1960, married and moved immediately to Thailand. This journey was my parents' first step away from India. They lived in a remote village while my father measured the Mekong River for "power potential." My mother arrived in her Banarasi silk sari by a tortuous route: first an overnight train took her from Bangkok north to Ubon, then at Ubon the jeep my father had been assigned rumbled and rattled for at least two hours over the two-rut road, over the wooden-slat bridges with no sides, over the billowing dirt to the village of Mukdahan. Mom remembers alighting and looking at her small purse mirror and finding she was completely covered in fine red dirt.

In Mukdahan, my mother had an *iya* to help care for my brother, Sandeep, born a year later, and myself the next year. The iya taught her to make Thai fried rice, which Mom still makes with flair. Beside the rice she placed a wedge of lime and a fresh, crisp stalk of green onion with three inches of green purposefully not trimmed to enliven the color of the platter. The crisp onions provided a satisfying crunch after bites of rice, and there was always a fan of cucumber slices and tomatoes nestled alongside the rice for an extra kick of flavor.

I always imagined that Mom did not cook much. She, also, was young and in a new culture. Now I know that for the first full month in the village, while my mother wrote frantic letters back home to India to get recipes from my grandmother, my father cooked his version of chicken curry every night. The spices of Thailand fit Indian dishes well, for the most part. The Thais used more lemongrass and ate more soups, but many of their spices overlapped. As letters arrived from India, Mom produced dal, chutney, vegetables with cumin—as she named the dishes recently, I looked at my recipe file and felt a jolt as I noted the same five recipes I first began to cook when newly married. She went home to India for three months to give birth to her first child, my brother, Sandeep, and to be near my grandmother while doing so. Then she returned with my dad to Thailand.

In the spring of the next year my father was seen carrying a brass candelabrum in the shape of a royal Thai boat through the marketplace. Its tipped-up end waved back and forth under his arm, following the motion of his hips as he weaved between stalls creating a wake for my pregnant mother to move through. Later, the candelabrum would become a family treasure and grace a piano top in Kansas and, even later, a table in my Missouri home. But in 1962, in the Southeast Asian heat, my parents forgot it in their flat as they hurried to the hospital for my birth. After I was born, my parents moved back to India again for one year. Recipes with estimated amounts of ginger, cardamom, or cloves no longer needed to be posted via international mail between my grandmother and mother. In India, there was always a cook.

❖ ❖ ❖

SIPRA'S THAI FRIED RICE (*KHOW PAT* FROM THE VILLAGE OF MUKDAHAN)

Serves 4

2 tablespoons vegetable oil
1 teaspoon Accent (premade seasoning found in grocery stores)
1 bay leaf
2 cups long-grain rice, cooked
1 tablespoon Worcestershire sauce
1 bunch green onions, washed and sliced
4 boiled eggs, cut up
½ pound medium tail-on shrimp, peeled and deveined
½ cup peas
½ medium cucumber, peeled and chopped
1 medium tomato, chopped

Garnish:
4 whole stalks of green onion, cut to leave 2–3 inches of green stalk
½ medium cucumber, sliced
½ medium tomato, sliced
1 lime, cut in quarters

Cook rice, set aside. Sauté shrimp in oil until just cooked and lift out of oil with a slotted spoon. Set aside. Add Accent, chopped green onions, and bay leaf to hot oil and sauté for 1 minute. Next put in cooked rice. Stir to coat grains. Add salt to taste. Add Worcestershire sauce. Add eggs and shrimp and gently stir. Arrange khow pat on plates with alternating slices of tomato and cucumber on one side, and a length of green onion and a lime wedge on the other. Serve with soy sauce.

Little India

This having-a-cook idea was added to the list of all tantalizing Indian things I could just remember but which were out of my reach by the age of eight: sidewalks full of people who looked like me, billboards full of movie stars with chocolate-brown eyes, ceiling fans, tea served on marble verandas. None of these were part of Kansas life. In the course of a regular day, I rarely even saw other Indians. Once in a while I glimpsed a few at my parents' parties or on one of our occasional shopping trips to Kansas City two hours away; in the city I was always alert for sightings.

I would always take immediate covert action to cross the path of an Indian family if I saw one in a Kansas City store. I wanted to poke my dad in the ribs, tug my mother's sleeve. Suddenly, there were *others*. But the recipients of my glee looked uninterested. Perhaps a child darting in their path and glancing at their bone structure (were they Bengali? South Indian?) was humdrum. Really, it was a good thing I didn't leap upon them and begin quizzing them on where they lived, went to school, and what they thought of Kansas. But the adults did not show interest in each other, did not even say hello—in Pittsburg Mom would have at least said *hello*. I tried to subdue my reaction, I tried to be as nonchalant as the rest of them, but I would still cross the other family's path at least five times. After the first startled look, the other mother tried not to make eye contact.

All things Indian intrigued me, though, most of all the religion that seemed to exist only there. So I began my campaign. On one long stretch of a Sunday in Kansas when my parents were reading *Time* magazine and the newspaper in bed, I climbed up between them and began asking if we could go to India. I gave them an eight-year-old's strongest case: "I want to know my grandparents."

But my unspoken wish to know of a religion that my parents never explained was just as strong. In Kansas, God was everywhere, I learned, but without further instructions he was hard for me to find. My friends in Kansas had a network of adults that seemed to have a precise story about God. I yearned for such a map.

When my mother and father arrived in Chicago in 1963, Mom brought her native dress, her lightly accented British English, a way of carrying herself and inclining her head a little to the right when greeting other Indians, a taste for the spices of India, and religious customs instilled as a child but hard to explain to children in Kansas. In India, religious customs were embedded in everyday rituals, in the types of foods eaten, in the way my parents were taught to greet others, in private home meditations and public festivals. Religion shaped my parents' world but they had no formal teacher. Without the cultural backdrop of India, the facts of their beliefs were hard to pin down.

Another reason for my lack of a map was also at the heart of a divide between East and West in the way scriptures were taught. Christian doctrine was well documented and spread throughout the known world via the printing press after Johannes Gutenberg's first Bible appeared in 1452, with forty-two lines per page. Its tenets were in plain sight. In fact, the visual dimension trumps everything in Western culture: knowledge is based upon and validated by observation. Seeing is believing.

In the East, sound may be the noblest sense, as Guy Beck says in *Sonic Theology: Hinduism and Sacred Sound*. Verbal stories passed from teacher to individual student were and still are the primary means of scripture dissemination. Transmission of sacred power is not to be trusted to the written, a difficulty for a Kansas-raised Indian with nary a priest in sight.

There is a strong connection to sound in almost all religions, though. In fact, oral chants among different traditions such as Shintoist, Buddhist, Brahman, Muslim, and Hebrew as well as Western Gregorian reveal a striking similarity, Beck says: a one-note recitation that includes fluctuating pitch. The goal of sacred chanting is to uncover truth more quickly than is possible through text. No one in Kansas told me about the sonic nexus of Hindu thought; I did not know of the view of the universe as an emanation from cosmic sound or vibration or of individual salvation through the use of sonic techniques. I was unaware of the idea that sound is an eternal substance in itself, nor did I know that sound, including speech, language, and music, has divine origin.

What I did know was that my father had just received a phone call from his friend Santosh. His undulating speech created in me lethargy of motion. I was content to hear the tones of friendship, of deep bass Bengali conversation. For forty minutes, an unheard-of length of time on an expensive long-distance call, Baba sat on the floor tethered to the phone by its twisted, spiraling cord with his back to the wall in the narrow hall. The hot-water heater sat behind a wooden door just at his shoulder and gurgled occasionally as he talked. The two young Bengali men had been in engineering college together in Chicago in the late 1950s. They had lived in a rooming house, shared meals, sat outside on warm days along the curb, grinned into a camera at one point with youth and vigor. Santosh was not really my father's younger brother but I called him *Kaku*, Uncle. It was redundant to say Kaku-uncle, Uncle Uncle, I knew, but it amused everyone. Baba took the call with a chuckle in his voice, leaned against the closet door, and began to talk animatedly. Periodically he stretched out his legs, twisted the cord, and in general held me enthralled with his ease of conversation and languid posture.

Perhaps because of the call, or perhaps because my parents had been thinking along the same lines anyway, my request to go to India reaped a trip. It had been three years. I was five when I last visited in 1967, and here is what I could conjure of that visit: a ripe-fruit-and-dust aroma, a vision of hazy, stretched rice paddies seen from near my grandparents' house on top of Tagore Hill, the taste of sweet mango, and the feel of rattan under my fingertips in my grandmother's living room. India left me with a curious idea of blue mountains, sculpted tea plantations, palm fronds reflected in water canals. I felt again the bone-deep exhaustion of stepping out of the Delhi airport at 2:00 A.M. to catch a taxi to a hotel, and the spellbinding notion that a boy could be so anxious to eat that he would bite through bitter banana skin to reach fruit.

Once during my last trip to India, I sat alone, swinging my heels above a dark marble floor, contemplating mangoes. There was a large bowl of just-ripened fruit on the table. Light streamed in from the far windows, making the tabletop glow. I could hear occasional sounds coming from a nearby room, probably a kitchen, where the women were. An auntie had told me to try a mango and cut one up for me; I began with the end pieces. There are three types of pieces in a correctly sliced mango: two long, crescent-shaped pieces from the sides with skin on their borders; the flat seed in the middle piece surrounded with its fleshy fruit (*anhti* in Bengali); then the two remaining pieces from the short ends. She had created a pile of such pieces in a large bowl. So I began by pulling the end pieces through my lips, scraping the green-gold skin with my teeth. Next, I ate the side pieces and left the center anhti piece for last because it made a mess on my fingers that needed to be licked off. When I got to the anhti, I held the slippery, pulpy ends gingerly, trying not to push down too much with my fingers and make indentations in the flesh.

I made my way through many of the mangoes in the bowl—something my aunts and mother clucked over. By the end, I was a pulpy mess. My lips, the skin just under my bottom lip, and especially the skin at the corners of my mouth eventually became raw and puckered. My stomach ached. But I swung my feet, occasionally looking up from pulp carnage, my five-year-old's thoughts focused not on consequences but on sweet fruit, smooth pulp, and nothing so much as that.

While I was growing up, each visit to India added to my store of images: a married couple trundling along on a small motorbike, the wife's sari tucked safely out of the wheels; a man on a bicycle carrying bundles twice his width and height stacked on his head; an elephant with political signs hanging over his sides and a loudspeaker blaring a message. But in Kansas, my visions of the East existed indoors.

In Kansas, in fact, India was a closet. On and off for years I entered the small room to find another world. My memory is thus: I stand in my parents' large walk-in closet and on the left are all Mom's work clothes: pantsuits, jackets, blouses, a couple of shirts that say Lakeside Junior High across the front for game Fridays at the school where Mom teaches English. It feels like everything is taller than I am and the closet goes on forever. On the right are Baba's suits, belts, and ties, plus a row of brown or black shoes across the floor underneath. It is the back that beckons. There, textured cottons and cool silks that skim your skin hang in a row of saris.

She hangs them by design: the pressed cotton together, the heavy South Indian silk, the light printed silk, the embroidered. Mom has a preference for elegant colors: dark gold, soft pewter, shimmering soft ivory. Those, plus deep peacock colors, hang at eye level. I touch the sari borders with real gold or silver threads and pleat their stiffness. The borders are heavier than the silk, making the fabric drape along the body when worn.

I stare awhile. I brush through the borders, stopping at the fanciest. I imagine working the tiny patterns and move on. I pass quickly by the hot pink sari I hate—probably because my girlhood room was pink ruffled perfection and by age eleven I am so much more grown up. I get to what I secretly call the Mod-Squad sari, the one with beautiful medallions of gold worked into sheer black-green silk chiffon. When draped across the hips and brought up to the shoulder, this sari steals the show. No way will I be allowed to wear this one. I hold one layer of the fabric up and my jeans show through the material. I pull the black slip and the fitted blouse off the hanger. I slip on some of Mom's heels and begin to wrap myself in the six yards of fabric. In the end, I drape the *anchol* over my shoulder so the fall of the border luxuriously brushes the backs of my legs. I turn to the mirror, oblivious to my slightly pudgy waist, and see a queen.

India hid in other spots around our Kansas home. Soft embroidered shawls were folded in the linen closet next to bath towels. Fine gold necklaces and bangles nestled in red boxes with latches in bedroom dressers next to Timex watches. The air bounced when my father spoke with his accented English and smoothed into what seemed like a song when my parents spoke our native Bengali. In the kitchen, aroma was India's chariot. When Mom cooked, I thought of the statues I'd seen of Siva, dancing in a circle with his arms and legs spinning. The movements, the spices, released one kind of dance of life and, for me, a particular scent.

Back from school one day, I looked on from my perch on the counter, legs swinging. Mom was preparing food. Five spices—cardamom pod, cinnamon stick, whole clove, bay leaf, and dried red chili pepper—sizzled a bit in hot oil and a curl of smoke wafted up from a pan. The spices popped just long enough to flavor the oil, ensuring a proper richness to the taste of the dish. Before anyone could worry much about that curl of smoke, Mom put in chopped onions, covering the bottom of the pan, and they sizzled and sputtered as oil shot toward the inside of Mom's wrist. The anger of the oil always surprised me. But in the kitchen dance, Mom had already turned away. After a few moments, she tipped the pan, added a bit of sugar to the hot oil, and stirred to caramelize. "You must do this nicely," Mom said. "Wait until it is dissolved a bit." She stirred and immediately the onions became glossy. Only then did the protein go into the oil. Only after the flavors had told their story.

Mom put in ground meat. It browned and then she turned down the heat and stirred the mixture while cooking for fifteen minutes before she added enough water to cover and slowly simmered it dry. Casually, she asked questions as she stirred, arranged pots on different burners, began to peel potatoes that had been boiled and now cooled in their jackets.

"So what are you girls up to this week?"

She mashed the potatoes by hand with some ground dried ginger and salt. She formed a thin layer of potato over one palm, added a tablespoon of the meat mixture from the stove and one raisin, and sealed it up into an egg-shaped chop.

"How was your math test?"

I jumped down from the counter at this point and rolled the chops in beaten egg and then in bread crumbs before frying them. She put out cilantro chutney, and apple chutney for me, and arranged it on a platter.

I skipped bits about my day as we talked. Like the time I was walking with my friends on the school sidewalk. Leaves swirled at our feet. Geography was next for me after lunch and I thought about how pleasant it was to sit and listen to the cadence of Mr. Newcombe's voice. He had a red mustache that curled up, red hair that bristled up, and an openness around his eyes. It was as if he wouldn't mind going to some of the places we talked about in class. I liked that about him. When we went to India, the world opened its arms and beckoned. My friend Kathy shuddered the last time my family left for a month to visit India in the summer.

"I wouldn't want to miss everything," she said to me.

As we went into the school, a boy in front of me turned as we swung toward the door. His lip curled up and his eyes narrowed.

"You worship cows."

His voice was loud and scoffing. I felt exposed and frozen. There was a heavy weight in my chest that felt something like anger. I wanted an easy, flip answer, and nowadays I have one: Indians don't worship cows—they respect life in all forms, not just human life. Instead, I curled my fist at my side and squeezed. My glare was double trouble. We walked as a group into the school.

Though I had time to tell my mother this, I did not, and she did not know to ask.

TIME TO CHAT CHOPS (GINGER MASHED POTATOES WITH SAVORY FILLING)

Makes about 12 chops

4 potatoes, boiled in their jackets and set aside to cool (these can be
    boiled a day ahead and refrigerated)
salt to taste, about 1 teaspoon
dry ginger powder to taste, about 1 teaspoon

Filling:
2 tablespoons oil
small piece of cinnamon stick
3 whole cardamom pods
3 whole cloves
1 small bay leaf
½ large onion, chopped
½ pound ground meat (beef or lamb)
¼ teaspoon cayenne pepper (or more, to taste)
1 inch of mashed fresh ginger
1 clove garlic

2 eggs, beaten, set aside
1 cup fine bread crumbs, set aside

Filling: Heat 2 tablespoons oil in saucepan; when hot, add cinnamon stick, cardamom, cloves, and bay leaf. Let sizzle for 10 seconds, add chopped onion, and fry until onions begin to turn brown at the edges. Add ground meat and brown. Add cayenne pepper, ginger, and garlic. Stir-fry for a few minutes. Add just enough water to cover and simmer until dry, stirring occasionally (about 20 minutes).

Wrapping: Beat 2 eggs in a shallow bowl and set aside. Pour bread crumbs into another shallow bowl and set aside. Peel potatoes and mash them with a fork or potato masher. They will not be perfectly smooth. Add salt and ginger and mix well. Flatten a layer of mashed, spiced potato mixture on your palm; add about 2 tablespoons of filling and 1 raisin. Close potato mixture around filling, adding more potato to the top to close if needed. Form egg-shaped ovals; roll chops in beaten egg and then roll in bread crumbs. Place on a flat plate or cookie sheet, ready to fry. Heat 1–2 inches of oil in a small wok or small, deep frying pan and fry chops until golden brown, turning to get evenly browned. Lift out of the hot oil when browned and place on a paper towel. Remove to a serving dish and serve warm with chutney.

DHONAE CHATNI (CILANTRO CHUTNEY)

Makes about ¾–1 cup

> 2 bunches fresh green coriander, rinsed and chopped, removing most
>   of the stems except the most tender
> 1 fresh, hot green chili, chopped
> 2 tablespoons lemon juice
> ½ teaspoon salt
> ½ teaspoon ground roasted cumin seeds
> black pepper to taste

Combine all ingredients in a blender until it forms a thin paste. Serve in a small bowl.

APPLE CHATNI (APPLE CHUTNEY)

Makes about 2 cups

4 apples, peeled and chopped (can add ½ cup chopped dried apricots
  and peaches if desired)
1 teaspoon either *kalo jeera*, which can be found at Indian groceries,
  or black mustard seeds
1 whole dried red pepper, broken
2 tablespoons concentrated tamarind paste
¾ cup sugar (or more to taste)
cayenne pepper to taste

Heat 2 tablespoons oil in the bottom of a saucepan and when hot add kalo
jeera or black mustard seeds and dried red pepper and fry until it sizzles.
Add peeled and chopped apples. Add other fruit if desired. Cover and cook
on medium-low heat. Stir occasionally until apples are soft. Add tamarind
paste, sugar, and cayenne to taste. Cook and stir until sugar is dissolved and
mixture thickens. Chutney will thicken further as it cools.

Journey

We went by car, plane, taxi, and train. We used every mode of transportation except those by sea to get my family of four from Kansas to Bengal. By the end of it, my parents were closing their eyes to ward off the monotony, but on that train to Bihar at the age of eight, I felt life rock and clack into my very bones and take shape as one great sweeping moment passing through me into an unmannered fantastic world.

At first, though, it was a very slow sweep.

It was an epic trip, the result of my hope to visit my grandparents and secret wish to get to the bottom of religion, and of my parents' own desire to go home. It had been three years since our last visit. From Pittsburg, Kansas, we traveled two and a half hours by car to Kansas City, then one hour to Chicago by plane, then seven hours by another plane to Munich, where we waited four hours to board a third plane for the six-hour trip to New Delhi. After we arrived at 2:00 A.M., we took a morning flight to Kolkata. There, in the largest city of my ancestral state of Bengal, we waited until the next day to venture to Howrah Station for our overnight train journey to Ranchi, in the state of what was then Bihar (now Jharkhand). I filled the five-plane, twenty-two-and-a-half-hour trip from Kansas to Bengal by watching movies using little plastic earphones, fiddling with the radio channels, and making trips to the metal bathrooms with accordion-looking doors on the flights. I was awakened for breakfast when it was suddenly morning. Breakfast was a roll, a small foil-wrapped wedge of Indian cheese, and fruit. Having no Cheerios or Cap'n Crunch on offer made me pause with interest, and slight melancholy, as I gazed at the tray.

Even at the time, I wanted to overlook all that monotony. But the train was another thing entirely. We were all a little transit-befuddled in Kolkata on the way to Howrah Station, a name I have always thought sounded like *howling*, like the din of all the bustle echoing through the chambers of the station itself. I remember seeing a small, pained-looking flower pushing its way up through a sidewalk crack as we approached the station and thinking that one more trample would destroy the petals for good. I stumbled as I watched it, then decided to look directly into my father's back to keep steady amid the hiss of steam, the slapping of hundreds of leather sandals on concrete, and the chattering of myriad voices. I jerked at the staccato of partial phrases in Hindi, Bengali, Urdu, and sometimes English. The vendors holding full trays of tea, samosas, and other treats that yelled for attention seemed almost soothing in the din. I wanted to be involved with everything. I was delighted with the crowds, the noise, the commotion, though my parents, burdened with keeping two children from wandering off, were less so. Once I made the mistake of looking over my shoulder into a train car while walking forward on the platform and got separated from my family until I caught at the back of my dad's coat.

I got a glimpse into the second-class cars where the compartments had six bunks. As my mother herded us toward the correct first-class berth, I caught sight of third class, where there were only chairs, no beds. I was fascinated by the people packed in everywhere in those cars, even standing in the tiny hall by the toilets where the floor would gyrate and bounce with the curves of the track when the train moved. The passengers had baskets with them full of food from home in round stainless steel food tins called tiffins, and the women were dressed in what I thought must be their best because they shimmered with gilded fabric and glass bangles. There were sounds of chatting, happy strangers on a journey. There was even a bride, still in her red wedding sari, with henna designs on her hands and feet. The cramped conditions didn't seem to bother anyone, and to me it looked like a celebration.

Stepping high into the skinny door of the train, we shuffled bags, squeezed around each other, and closed the door after us, muffling much of the platform sound. When we first boarded, the curtains in the main walkway were all open, but it would appear warren-like later, after the curtains had been drawn. In our compartment, four berths protruded horizontally like shelves from the wall, two on each side. The beds had individual fabric curtains on rings you could slide closed for privacy. At the end of the beds was a long curtain that closed off our compartment from the central walkway. I was on top since I could scramble up easier than my parents. Brushing dark red fabric as I walked the hushed aisle, I saw little piles of the round tiffins, square boxes wrapped in brown paper and tied with strings that I was sure contained sweets, and a child's rucksack with blue and red patches scattered on the berths. Looking down the narrow, dim hall, I didn't see or hear anyone else. Though my parents breathed a sigh of relief to be out of the crowds and in relative privacy, I felt blocked off from the action.

Then my dad cracked open the window.

"*Gorum chai! Gorum chai!*" A vendor's piercing singsong entered the car. He supported a tray of steaming cups of tea with a strap around his neck as he moved down the platform, his voice undulating. Hands stuck out all down the train for steaming cups of tea with milk and sugar. I stuck mine out, too, at my mother's nod, and found myself choosing a *shingara* from the next vendor. Some of the flaky crust and spicy potatoes of the shingara fell onto my blouse as I watched the steam on the platform blow densely, then clear from the front of the train. People seemed to drift through the billows. I wiped my window and leaned forward. A woman in a brilliant pink sari, holding a small case on her head, wafted through. Her straight back and gliding step were as beautiful as anything I had ever seen, but she went completely unnoticed in the manic scene of Howrah. She drifted through and was gone.

As I watched through the window, a family of three arrived at the compartment across the narrow hall and immediately started arranging their beds. The hush inside the train car was momentarily disturbed. Then it was time to depart, and the train jerked slightly, disengaging from its moor, and coasted for just a moment, causing a thrill of anticipation to edge down my spine. The engine then expulsed a great gusting black cloud, with a noise like a whale clearing its blowhole, and proceeded to churn up a fierce head of steam, creating even more billows along the platforms. I wanted to lean out the window to watch, to smell the coal dust, to feel the gathering wind. As the rhythmic click of the tracks began and then got quicker and quicker, I settled for leaning back on my bunk and eventually felt myself relax.

I watched as the train moved out of the clutter and confusion and charm of Kolkata with its sharp-edged smells, fantastic wares, banging, clanging market streets, and beggars. As the train left the station, the coconut milk vendors continued to make small holes in the hairy brown shells for straws, and drink wallahs (vendors) with other beverages sat at little tables and swished glasses in the tubs of water by their feet to make them "clean" for the next customer. A small boy scuffed along a side street. No one even glanced up at the passing train.

Market stalls began to rocket past. I watched the scene blur as an auto rickshaw dodged a pothole. Three-wheeled motorized rickshaws with their pull-up black tops and clear plastic windows darted everywhere. The air was filled with their exhaust and blaring horns. The city's choked avenues were another world swarming with people and pushcarts, round-edged cars like my grandfather's and sleek foreign cars. Even the huge billboards showing the latest movie stars in various action stances began to recede with the rest of the city.

We moved toward hazy hills. For me, the metaphorical journey home at dinnertime in Kansas met the physical one with this trip, the first trip to India I would remember clearly. All the times my mother had produced Indian meals back in Kansas to tie our little family to this homeland culminated in this moment as my head rolled against the back of the red leather seat in rhythm with the dry sound of metal surfaces endlessly colliding on the track. At eight years old, heading on a train toward an undefined place, my head rocking a little, I felt I was neither here nor there, in limbo between loss and anticipation.

Later, I found sleeping on the train much better than on the plane. First a waiter brought around the linens, a bottom sheet and a short blanket. Then we pulled the curtains closed and stretched out. The swaying of the train made my torso shift from side to side and sleep was possible.

The morning sun came up as we passed through smaller villages and bigger towns. I watched market stalls come into view again. The stalls for small schools looked pathetic, forlorn to my Western eye: not real schools, but what villagers could afford. In Kolkata, there were bricks and mortar and gated grounds for such enterprises. Here I saw signs reading "College" hanging over storefronts not much bigger than a sweet stall.

After we got off the overnight train around 8:00 A.M., the world outside the window slammed back into focus: the milling crowd, the platform, the hullabaloo. I needed propping up and leaned heavily against my mother, holding a piece of her sari. The Ranchi station was a smaller, somewhat quieter version of Howrah but still had drifting billows of steam. The puffs of white smoke shaded darker and blacker near the engine and I momentarily lost a group of people walking in front of us. I wondered if I could ever glide through the mist, graceful, and still turn up where I was supposed to be going. Would my silhouette be beautiful flashing through the mottled air? Not wanting to risk it, I decided to follow my parents very closely.

Ranchi had been a summer escape for both Indians and the British in the time of the Raj. It was known for its waterfalls, its distant hills, and for being a center of centuries-old Bihari customs and worship. Gautama Buddha had been englightened in this state, at Bodh Gaya in the modern city of Gaya, and had launched a world religion. But I knew it for my grandparents' home, Rani Villa.

My grandfather, Amiya, brought the car. He emerged out of the crowds at the terminal station, dapper and keen. His body leaned slightly forward as he looked for us, and then everyone was speaking at once. My father's face broke into a large smile, Mom looked happy. No one hugged—public displays were not the thing in my family, though we felt warmth in the reunion.

There was some talk about the *bandh*, the strike of all transport drivers, but in the end it just made the traffic lighter for us. That day, as Dadu passed through the market area of Ranchi and across town to Rani Villa, I saw the school signs again. Computer Technology College, one said, the Finest Tools. It was wedged between a sweet shop and one selling baskets full of colored beads. There was a slender boy inside, head bent over a book and paper, a pencil in his hand. He was in blue shorts, a white shirt, and a thin tie. Two little girls swung by wearing navy-blue pinafores with white blouses and socks. I caught sight of people stopping by the sweet shops and taking away boxes tied with string for their families, and stray dogs deftly weaving between legs to catch anything that dropped.

As my grandfather made his way toward his home, I did not think of Kansas. Though this place, this trip, would make sense of the many differences I found in my family routine back in Pittsburg, what I noticed was the melon colors of verandas along the road. The houses were flat topped and I got the idea that the muddy earth here surged each monsoon and a house burst forth with fresh paint, straight and very tall, in a place where only the peepul trees were tall. With time, mold and moss would creep over the pale pinks and butter yellows of the plaster walls until, grayish and mottled, the walls blended the space between the soil and sky, as if a charcoal artist had just smudged their edges. The houses, with names like Purdeshi ("Foreigner"—owned by a neighbor whose family came here two generations ago), Rani Villa (named for my grandmother, Rani), and other names depicting gardens or flowers, were not in open view like at home but were walled and had wrought-iron gates on the drives and the courtyard doors. Fuchsia bougainvillea, white jasmine, gold-green mangoes, and yellow-brown bananas grew with abandon and were captured within; Rani Villa's closed front gate cinched in a bouquet.

Kamla, my grandparents' housekeeper, and her children waited for us at the door. She stood with the tail of her sari pulled around to the front and clasped in her folded hands in a pose I remember from all my trips to this house. She smiled her sweet smile as we pulled up. After the bustle of getting out of the car, of transporting suitcases inside, of taking off our shoes in the vestibule and entering through the double wooden doors, Kamla dipped away into the kitchen to tend the coal *unoon* that heated a kettle. She emerged a short time later, after we had settled in my grandmother's living room, carrying hot milky tea and diamond-shaped *mishtis*, chhana-based sweets with wafer-thin silver foil pressed on top. I suddenly realized that this was the basis for the way tea was served at home. Mom always brought it out already milky and sweet for Indian guests. In my grandparents' living room, Kamla made another round with *rosogollas*, literally "round balls in syrup," which quickly became my favorite.

Kamla's fingers fluttered a bit as she arranged the tray, as if getting this right was important. I suppose our visits were rare enough that it seemed so. I looked around the room at framed black-and-white photos, at a calendar tacked to one wall with a smiling baby illustration—Krishna, I decided, because of the "holy" blue color used—at a simple painting of a tree in its four seasons of foliage in a cream-colored chipped frame. The house was spare and had an aura of practicality, each piece of furniture useful and suitable for the climate, made out of cane and thin fabric cushions, the rugs scattered and easily rolled, the windows with hinged panes that were opened or closed depending on the heat of the day. There was an outside stair, however, that seemed magical to me. It led to the flat roof on which Tagore Hill, named for the Bengali poet and Nobel Laureate Rabindranath Tagore, could be clearly seen as well as acres of rice paddies fading off into the distance.

Didu's home had its own fruit trees, and she grew mangoes, the kind that luxuriate in summer heat. Fruit was so abundant you had only to go outside in the right season and pluck your treat from the tree. *This* was why Mom had planted a peach tree in Kansas when no one else in the neighborhood tried. In Ranchi, tree branches were so laden with fruit at certain times of year that they arched over Dadu's goldfish pond. These mangoes did not come by refrigerated truck from Mexico to ripen off the vine like they did in the Pittsburg grocery, when you could get them. Their pulp was smooth as silk, not fibrous, and could almost be scooped out of their skin with a spoon like pudding. We never got as far as using spoons, however, when eager fingers would do. I imagine mangoes continue to blush—green-gold, persimmon—during their season behind Rani's kitchen, that they hang, pendulous and still, for chattering monkeys or determined humans to pick at peak flavor.

A veranda protected Rani Villa from the relentless sun, and there, Kamla brought me four-o'clock-tea the next day. The fan swirled the air from the ceiling, smooth tiles cooled my feet, and I was rapt away.

SHINGARA (VEGETABLE OR MEAT PASTRY)

Makes about 12 shingaras

Preheat oven to 400°F.
Or, pour 1½ inches of oil in a small, deep frying pan.

Filling:
3 medium potatoes, peeled and chopped into 1-inch cubes
1–2 teaspoons salt
1 teaspoon ground coriander
¼ cup raisins
¼ cup cashews (optional)

1 tablespoon vegetable oil

2 teaspoons cumin seeds
1 large onion, finely chopped
¼ cup green peas
½-inch piece of fresh ginger root, peeled and grated
¼ teaspoon cayenne (or to taste)
2 teaspoons fresh lime juice (lemon juice also works)
2 green chilies, very finely chopped
¼ cup fresh cilantro leaves, finely chopped
1–2 cloves garlic, mashed or finely chopped
1 cup small cauliflower florets, cooked (optional)

Boil the peeled, cubed potatoes until soft. Drain. Mash potatoes against the side of a mixing bowl with a fork and add salt, ground coriander, raisins, and cashews. Set aside. In a small pan, heat the oil. When hot, add the cumin seeds. After 4–5 seconds, add the onion. Stir-fry for 2 minutes, then add peas, ginger, cayenne, lime juice, green chilies, cilantro, garlic, and cauliflower. Take pan off heat and mix well. Add potato mixture and mix.

Pastry:
1½ cups all-purpose flour (*maida* in Indian food stores)
½ teaspoon salt
4 tablespoons vegetable oil
4–5 tablespoons water

In a medium-sized mixing bowl, mix flour, salt, and oil with your fingers until it resembles coarse crumbs. Gradually add water until you have a stiff dough. Turn the dough out onto a clean surface and knead for about 10 minutes. Divide dough into 8 balls and cover with a clean towel. One at a time, roll each ball into a 7-inch round. Cut this in half with a knife. Lift the end of one half and form a cone, making an overlapping seam and using a little water on the tip of your finger to hold it together. Fill the cone with about 3 tablespoons of potato mixture. Close the open top edges together with another overlap, place on a baking sheet, and then press the seam down with a fork.

Reduce preheated oven temperature to 350°F. Bake about 45 minutes or until the shingaras are crispy and a uniform light brown color.

Or, heat 1–2 inches of oil in a small, deep frying pan over medium heat. Place as many shingaras in hot oil as the pan will hold in a single layer. Fry slowly, turning pieces often until all are golden brown and crisp. Drain on a paper towel.

Serve with coriander chutney, sweet mango chutney, or any of your other favorites.

> Shingaras can also be stuffed with minced lamb (or beef):
> 2–3 tablespoons oil
> 3 whole cloves
> ½ stick cinnamon
> 3 whole cardamom pods
> 1 bay leaf
> 1 dried red chili pepper
> 1 medium-sized onion, chopped
> ¼ teaspoon sugar
> ½ pound minced meat
>
> ½ teaspoon powdered ginger, or about 1 inch of fresh ginger root, mashed
> ¼ teaspoon cayenne
> ¼ teaspoon fresh garlic, mashed
> ½ of a medium tomato, cut in half
> salt to taste
> ¼ teaspoon garam masala (optional)
> ½ cup green peas (optional)

Cover the bottom of a heavy pan with vegetable oil and heat. When hot, drop in the cloves, cinnamon stick, cardamom, bay leaf, and dried red chili and sizzle for about 30 seconds. Add the onions. When the onions begin to brown, add the sugar and stir to dissolve. Add in the ground lamb or beef. Stir-fry the meat with the onions until the meat is completely browned. Add the remaining spices. Lower heat, add a little water if necessary, and fry until the meat is well coated with the spices. Add tomato and garam masala. Add about 1 cup water and green peas if desired. Loosely cover the pan and simmer until mixture is almost dry. Remove whole spices before filling the shingaras.

ROSOGOLLAS (CHEESE BALLS IN SYRUP—A BENGALI SPECIALTY)

Makes 12 pieces

Use two stockpots large enough to accommodate the finished rosogollas, as they will expand to about double the volume while cooking in the syrup.

chhana from ½ gallon whole milk [see recipe on page 13]
1½ cups sugar
10 cups water

After the chhana has hung to dry and has been kneaded, divide it into 12 equal parts and roll these firmly into smooth balls so they stay together. Mix the sugar and water together to make syrup in the large stockpot and heat over medium heat to bring to a boil. Drop the chhana balls into the heated syrup and cook for 45 minutes. Syrup will thicken slightly as you cook the rosogollas. Turn off the heat. The rosogollas will be a little spongy, but they will become less so after they are refrigerated. Serve chilled.

Remember, if the rosogollas don't turn out exactly right, if they are brittle or oddly shaped, try breaking them into small pieces and put them into payesh [page 160] alongside the rice or vermicelli noodles, almonds, and raisins. Enjoy!

BADAM BURFI (SWEET ALMOND CONFECTION)

Makes 20 pieces

1 cup almonds, finely ground
⅓ cup whole milk
¾ cup sugar
⅛ teaspoon ground cardamom
2 tablespoons butter

Grease a 6 x 6-inch shallow pan with butter. In a medium-sized saucepan, blend the ground almonds with the milk. Add the sugar and stir vigorously for 2 minutes. Place on stove and cook and stir the almond mixture over medium heat for about 5 minutes. Add the 2 tablespoons butter and continue to stir constantly until the mixture thickens and starts to leave the sides of the pan (about 6 minutes). Add the cardamom powder and remove pan from heat. Stir the mixture vigorously with a spoon for 3 minutes until it has the consistency of bread batter. Pour about ¼ inch of the almond mixture into the prepared greased pan. Smooth the surface with the back of a spoon. Let cool for about 20 minutes. Cut into diamond shapes. Cool completely and store pieces in an airtight container, where they will last 1 week, or 2 months if refrigerated.

Table Grace

My parents relished eating in the Indian way at times, taking care
to use only the ends of their fingers. Nothing is as clean as the
human body, no utensil washed indifferently, certainly. The tac-
tile feel of food on the fingers, too, was part of the experience. There was a
proper way to do this in my family: the fingertips were drawn together with
the thumb to form a pincer of sorts. Food was never allowed to creep above
the first knuckle, and bits of food were all consumed from the inside of the
fingertips. No debris was apparent on the upper fingers or left for the next
bite. The ritual of hand eating was not something I practiced in Kansas, and
when I met my thirteen cousins at Pishima's house, this became a liability.

My father's oldest sister's house was about a two-hour trip from my grandparents' home in Ranchi over a road that spiraled around hills and villages.
My cousin-brother, Jogu, came to pick us up and drove confidently over the
bumpy, curving route. When we passed near a game reserve, he said there
was a tiger living there. I looked into the swaying tree limbs and squinted at
the dusty leaves but saw nothing beyond the perimeter forest.

Then the land opened up a bit and I arrived at Hazaribagh for the first time
since I was a baby. We walked inside Pishima's three-story U-shaped house,
built with verandas on each floor facing the interior courtyard, and trundled
up to the second floor. There were no chairs in the room so I kneeled on a

carpet and looked all around. There seemed to be a sea of boy faces. Only three of my cousins were girls, and they were older and married now. "Hi, what are your names?" I grinned and sat forward. As soon as the words were out, I realized I would never remember all the names.

Several pairs of eyes blinked and smiles broke out on one or two faces. My American accent made them speechless. They were: Shobhan, Tarun, Abhik, Prabir, Samir, Sudhir, Sridhar, Shubir, and Amitabha. Of course, their pet names, the names the family called them, were different: Jogu, Babu, Gopal, and more. It became quiet again. My brother, Sandeep, shuffled his feet. I was struck by the fact that I had never been in a room full of Indian children before. For once, I looked much like those around me, except for being a girl. Everyone had wavy black hair, chocolate eyes, and strongly arched eyebrows. I barely knew these boys, but I was comfortable.

Then one boy asked if we liked to sing. They all sang. Several played the tabla, or drums, or the harmonium. Since television was not a national pastime yet in India, music was the primary form of entertainment in most homes. I felt fearful that I would be required to burst forth in song to prove my family membership. The only Bengali song I knew was what my grandfather taught me as a joke: "*Ami Bangla boosta pari, kinto bolta pari na!*" Even a tabla accompaniment would not help with that declaration (I understand Bengali but cannot speak it!). Telling them I didn't sing baffled them. Conversation stalled but they didn't press the song issue. I was serenely happy. There was no need to fear. Cousins, I think. Just like my friends' families in Pittsburg.

I found that our family had only a few girls. I was startled by this thought. My mother's brothers all had boys. My father's siblings had mostly boys, fully evidenced in Hazaribagh. I knew there was also a cousin-sister in Kolkata named Indrani, and one in Patna called Suchitra. In Kansas, there were only my brother and I, one of each, and I thought that was the way of things. Isolated in Kansas, with no one talking about cousin-brothers and cousin-sisters, I had no idea I was so unusual.

Later that day Jogu came in and took me for a ride on his motorbike. His hair was very tall and frizzy and it got bigger as we rode. I saw Jogu many times over the years. He became a Rotarian later in life and visited the United States. I saw him on all my visits to India, including one in which his wife made *oothappam*, a lovely dal and rice-based pancake from the south of India. I've had oothappam since with coconut clinging to its bottom and another version with tomatoes and carrots mixed into the batter. To make it, you soak rice and lentils for several hours and then grind them into flour before making the batter. That day, *Boudi* (older cousin-brother's wife) made it in quick fashion with semolina and onions and served it with cilantro chutney. It was perfection.

But well before then, sitting behind Jogu on the moped, I was thrilled to be bumping along on the dirt road waving at cousins. It was amazing to see the sheer numbers of family members. Eventually, we came back to the house. The central courtyard was not fancy, but the arms of the house swept you inside. Broad-leaved plants grew here and there. There was a row of archways. Upstairs, the openings were plain, but loggias remained. The walls were white and peeling.

My father's oldest sister had his face. I peeked at it as Pishima settled herself on a daybed. Despite being nearly seventy and having thirteen children, she had smooth skin and just a few grooves on her forehead and beside her eyes. Her eyes were kind. She wore a white sari with a red embroidered border on the bottom, and when she walked she rocked a little from hip to hip. I was intimidated by her and by *Pishaemoshai* (father's oldest sister's husband), tall, thin, and austere. They asked me to sit with them and then patted me on the leg and shoulder. They offered me sweets, the Bengali kind I loved, made with chhana. This ritual of sweets and tea was the mark of all good Bengali hosts—this offering showed caring, love, and generosity. I grew round over the course of our visit to India by all the love shown in this way. Sometimes my grandparents went around to several friends' homes in an evening. After two or three sweets at each home, it was easy to see how this happened. Pishima, like all the other people we met, was inordinately pleased that I ate the sweets with such relish, as if this proved my belonging more than anything else. No one asked me a question, though, and so I said little.

After some time, Pishima called us upstairs for dinner. The steps up to the eating area seemed worn with age and the slapping of many cousin-feet up to the table. I loved the feel of the smooth marble, so slippery that I touched the rough stucco walls for balance on the way up. At the top of the stairwell, against the waist-high wall that overlooked the courtyard, was a large clay pot of cool water. I trailed my fingers along the texture of the clay, earthy brown and tamarind colored, and I noted the ladle and the metal cup next to it for drinking. The veranda was deep and there were flat benches along the wall. Some of the seats were woven rattan and some were covered in bright cloth. We passed the place for washing hands and walked into a square room. We sat at a table that practically filled the space. The oldest cousins had first shot at a seat, while the younger ones lined the walls. My mother and I sat as well, but no other women were in the room. The Indian custom of the males eating first, then children, then women, was suspended because we were from far away.

At home, my brother used me as his food taster. When Mom put a bowl of something new on the table, Sandy peered at it cautiously without moving toward it in any way. As the new dish made its way around the table, he watched my face. I liked eating almost anything, but he was picky, and I knew what he might or might not like. When I thought he'd like something I nodded my head almost imperceptibly. Heroically, I never misled him.

Our system did not work at Pishima's house. Sandy was down the same side of the table as I was, small behind the bulk of a larger male, so I could not beam across emergency food-tasting results. *Thalas*, round metal plates with rims, were in front of each of us and a pile of rice shaped like an upside-down ice-cream cone was in the middle of each one. Some fried cauliflower nestled beside the rice. Round *batis*, small flat-bottomed bowls, encircled the larger plate and held various foods: chutney, dal, another *tarkari* (vegetable), *maach* (fish), *mangsho* (meat), and *mishti doi* (sweet yogurt). It seemed a vast array compared to our one-vegetable, one-meat, one-starch meals in Kansas.

I saw no utensils, so I tried to imitate my mother, using just the ends of my fingers, deftly pulling a few grains of rice together along with a bit of dal or a piece of cauliflower. Next, Pishima brought in fish, mustard flavored and delicate, followed by a course of lamb curry. She smiled as she watched us eat and would take food only after serving everyone. At the end, we ate chutney, which completed the satisfying flavor medley of Pishima's meal.

I was not so lost in flavor that I missed all the eyes watching me eat. Boys who could not fit at the table lined the walls and they watched curiously, hands behind their backs or tucked into pockets. Occasionally my father made a comment and male guffaws rippled around the perimeter. Mom was at ease, but I felt a tightening ball inside my stomach and I hoped no one offered me a fork.

I would have died of embarrassment if this had happened. The family seemed thrilled to have us there but perplexed at my table customs. I did not eat this way at home, and they noticed my clumsy fingering. There might have been a little dal that crept above my first knuckle, close to the second. More food was brought in, and there were endless offers of more aromatic rice, more dal, more cauliflower, more potatoes.

Coming to such a place has a way of making you replace old ideas about yourself with something new. But to get anywhere, you have to let go of all the ideas, even the niggling ones, and see what comes. That day, as we pulled away I put my forehead against the window and watched my cousin-brothers wave. We had just made what was to be in coming years a traditional trek up to the rooftop. The photos show all of the cousins encircling us, with Pishima and Pishaemoshai in the middle. In subsequent visits over the next fifteen years, these cousins, along with their newly acquired spouses—Leela, Dheera, Deepa, Manju, Geeta, Mita, Sudeepa, Sharmila, Meeli—and children fill the camera lens and almost the entire rooftop for this same family pose. I was not as different as all that, I thought as we pulled away. I was not cut off from extended family. I felt tears coming because back in Kansas, there was only us around the table, and though I was proven wrong, I just knew I would never see those boys again.

COUSIN JOGU'S SAVORY OOTHAPPAM
(DAL AND RICE PANCAKE)

Makes 6 oothappams

1 cup Cream of Wheat
1½ tablespoons vegetable oil
pinch each of chana dal, urad dal, salt, and mustard seeds
1 medium onion, diced
1 green chili, chopped very finely
6 curry leaves
4 tablespoons fresh cilantro, chopped
1 tomato, chopped (optional)
1 carrot, finely chopped (optional)
2 cups water

roasted peanuts, chopped
1 tablespoon vegetable oil for griddle

Stir-fry the dry Cream of Wheat in a dry frying pan until the granules are light brown/golden. Remove them from the pan. Heat the oil in the pan, add the pinch of mustard seed, chana dal, urad dal, and 5–6 curry leaves. Brown the dal and add the diced onion. Fry until the onions become soft but not yet brown. Add the chili and optional chopped carrot and tomato. After 20 seconds add 2 cups water and salt to taste. When the water boils, add the Cream of Wheat and a few chopped roasted peanuts. Stir continuously until thick batter consistency is reached. Add oil to a heated griddle, ladle a large spoonful of batter onto the surface, and cook for 2 minutes before gently flipping to cook the other side. Serve with chutney if desired.

COUSIN JOGU'S SWEET OOTHAPPAM (DAL AND RICE PANCAKE)

Use the same recipe as above but do not add the onion or vegetables. Instead, before you flip the oothappam sprinkle shredded sweet coconut flakes over its surface, then turn the cake and cook until lightly browned. Or, try it with a mashed banana added to the batter.

PISHIMA'S PUNGENT JHALDAE MAACH (MUSTARD FISH)

1½ tablespoons mustard seed, ground into a paste with a little water
½ teaspoon turmeric
salt to taste
1 green chili, finely chopped
¼–½ teaspoon cayenne
1 cup water

1 tablespoon oil
1 small onion, sliced in long, thin strips

8 pieces fresh fish
1 green chili, finely chopped
1 cup water

Mix the mustard paste, turmeric, salt, green chili, and cayenne in a small bowl, add 1 cup of water, and set aside. Heat the oil in a frying pan, add the sliced onion, and stir-fry until the onions turn slightly brown. Push the onions to the side of the pan and drain the oil. Place fresh fish fillets on the surface. Pour the mustard paste mixture over the fish to cover. Cover and simmer until sauce is thick and fish is cooked through. Serve with rice.

6

Small Things Satisfied

Back from India, the four of us dropped back into routine. I found myself helping Mom with chops in the kitchen. Mom's cream and orange-trimmed curtains fluttered around a slice of backyard and I could see the honeysuckle bush nestled against my bedroom window. As always in the late afternoon, the tips of the branches gleamed gold and verdant tendrils grasped at the air like delicate fingers.

I hurried with my part of the chops, not really helping all that much, and left the kitchen. The humid press of clothing suctioning onto my skin after the air-conditioning felt good, despite all the Indian adults telling me it was bad to feel the heat, that the sun was to be avoided. But to me it felt like Rani Villa heat, like my grandparents' veranda at midday, like what we had just left again for years, and I found that I relished the hot Kansas sun at four o'clock, softened and less angry. The neighborhood girls appeared from out of their yards just as if I'd never been away and Susan, Kathy, and I plucked honeysuckle flowers, gently pulling the stamens to get at the tiny liquid drop poised on the end. Bee-hum made the surrounding air pulse: the effortless chant of small things. I had heard this hum at Rani Villa, and I heard it in Kansas: satisfaction in a vast realm right beneath our noses.

Our own bodies thrummed with the bees as we carefully pulled the tender, slightly rubbery, translucent stamens smoothly between our lips. As the sun warmed our necks, we looked cross-eyed at our fingers and concentrated on softly pinching the orange tips. The taste was fleeting-sweet and could be missed. There were so many flowers we did not fear the drowsily buzzing, satiated bees.

My father was mowing and dandelion fluff was smoothly drifting through the air. I looked up to see him pause and drink water in the Indian way: the rim of the glass never touching his lips, the liquid arcing through the air and hitting the back of his tongue. He swallowed and his strong neck convulsed. The timing of the act was impeccable. No dribbles marred his shirt as he turned the glass upright after the water was airborne. He then walked over and handed the remaining water to me and I tipped the glass while holding it slightly above my nose, trying to imitate his technique. I felt a burst of pride in the fact that my friends would never think to do this. They continually passed each other their Pepsis or Dr Peppers for a sip, gumming the straws or bottle tops without thought.

In India, my parents had cautioned us to not drink anything from street vendors unless it was from a coconut stall. The coconut vendor would puncture a round brown coconut husk and stick a straw through the opening. No need to do the water trick, as nothing needed washing. I watched as vendors of other drinks, like delicious salty or sweet yogurt *lassies*, put the used glasses in tubs of graying water at their feet once a customer was done. Lassies were a favorite of mine: lush and also light with froth, my favorite kind fruity and sweet. I would much rather have had a lassie. But even though I was young, I could see the wisdom of choosing a coconut drink.

In our backyard, I watched one friend's face when my father did the water trick on that hot, dry Kansas day when he had stopped mowing. I still felt such admiration for the feat—it showed cleanliness, consideration, and savvy—and I expected awe from my friend. But her look was different from admiration: something a little horrified but almost tender, like someone watching a quaint custom of the natives. The small thrum of contentment forming in my throat slowly constricted until I could not feel it at all.

To distract myself, I looked over at the clothesline, and remembering the birds, I put the glass down on the patio, wiping dribbles off my chin, and ran around the honeysuckle to check the hollow ends of the T-shaped pipe. The fat honeysuckle effectively blocked my view of the clothesline and for days I would forget about the birds that might nest there. But if the birds built a nest in the end of the pipe, the tiny offspring would totter off the edge in early bursts of independence and fall to their deaths. Fearing this, I checked now for the telltale gathering of twigs and straw debris. I had to stand three or four feet back to see that high but when I saw plant bits, I called my dad. He cut the mower engine off again, came over, and cleared them out of the end of the pipe. But it was a battle to keep the pipe bird-free. They were stealthy. It seemed as if one day there were a few twigs and the next a finished nest, with chirps echoing hollowly from inside.

When I was seven, birds got a thatch of twigs going before we noticed and later in the season, small baby birds dropped five feet to the grass and died. Yet there were never dead baby birds at the base of our trees. Was the lack of the rhythms and familiar chirping of other birds in nearby branches the reason the pipe children wandered? Were they dissatisfied? Pushed by a terrible karma? My mother's Pekingese, Sugar, drawn to the base of the clothesline, gently lifted the limp baby birds in her jaws, tasting what dogs love to taste, and their fragile translucent skin failed. My fingers had reached out to save the tiny creatures, and in jerks I pulled back. *No.* Then softly, *bad dog.*

As night crept in, there was no more bee dance. I went inside for bath and bed as the birds stopped flying. The tips of the honeysuckle raked the screen outside my bedroom window and shadows loomed, distorting the tender-leaved branches. One shadow flicked the bedroom wall. I waited under my sheets, unable to close my eyes. Something scraped across the mesh screen. I grew stiff lying in my twin bed with my legs straight out in front of me, my eyes on the window. There. Barely audible, a faint brushing sound scuttled along my nerves.

The round, plump honeysuckle bush had changed now: its familiar aura of bee hum that I shared with friends, gone, and I knew the dream would come. A feathery skip of the wind made me clench my fists. The delicate scratching noise was made by *a man and he would get in through the window and hold me with a knife at my neck at the bedroom door and my dad would wake up and I kept quiet so Baba wouldn't come down the hall because I was so afraid of what might happen to him and if I was quiet enough the man with the knife tight to my skin wouldn't know about everyone else in the house.* Night after night I had this dream and would go to bed crying until I finally, finally, told my mother and she patted my stiff knees and said *it is okay now.* And, it was. She somehow dispatched the horror of it with four words and I released the notion for a spell that if I tried hard enough I could protect my family from the outside world, could protect them from being pushed into acting in unpredictable ways. Even at eight, I knew India was suspect because of the stories about starvation there and a little-understood religion, and that any misstep of ours represented confirmation of our Kansas community's worst fears. I wanted those wolves of misunderstanding kept away.

MISHTI LASSIE (SWEET YOGURT DRINK)

Makes 1–2 drinks

1 ripe mango or banana or papaya, peeled and pureed
2 teaspoons honey or sugar (to taste)
¼ teaspoon saffron threads, steeped in 2 teaspoons hot water (optional)
1 cup water with ice
2 tablespoons lemon juice (to taste)
1 cup plain yogurt

Blend all of the above ingredients in an electric blender, crushing the ice. Lovely served chilled. Optional garnishes for each glass: ¼ teaspoon crushed pistachio nuts or a sprig of fresh mint.

NONTA LASSIE (SALTY YOGURT DRINK)

Makes 1 drink

1 cup plain yogurt
1 cup water with ice
salt to taste
fresh cilantro sprig (optional)

Blend the ingredients in an electric blender and serve. Garnish with a sprig of fresh cilantro if desired.

Indian Breads

When it was nearly five o'clock, I slipped back inside and heard a rolling pin slapping against the countertop as Mom shaped roti into exact rounds. She did not make these every day, so the rhythmic sounds of bread making were intoxicating. As M. F. K. Fisher says in *The Art of Eating*: "[Breadmaking is] . . . like a dance from some ancient ceremony. It leaves you filled with one of the world's sweetest smells . . . there is no chiropractic treatment, no Yoga exercise, no hour of meditation in a music-throbbing chapel that will leave you emptier of bad thoughts than this homely ceremony of making bread." It follows, then, that bread coincides closely with religion in most countries in the world. There are 250 references to it in the Bible alone. It is what feeds a nation, even rice-rich India.

There, breads run the gamut: *porota*, a fried bread stuffed with onion and potato; roti, a whole wheat staple made on a griddle without oil; *luchi*, puffy, flaky, and fried; naan, stretched to an elongated shape and slightly chewy; *dosa*, a thin crepe-like bread spread into a large circle; oothappam, somewhat like a pancake; and more.

In our house, Mom made two types most often: roti and luchi. For roti, Mom said, pinching off a one-inch piece of dough, "press and smooth the dough between your palms nicely. Only then are they ready to roll out." She placed the rolled rotis, a little overlapped, on the counter, then gingerly picked up one and placed it on the flat, heated iron pan for twenty seconds before I flipped it over. Next, I stepped up and placed the roti on the wire rack over the second burner and watched it puff up as Mom placed another on the flat pan. I turned the first bread, let it just barely brown in spots, pinched a side with tongs, and placed it on a round clay serving plate. The bread evaded the tongs a bit, causing me to snap them together in missed grabs until I snared a tiny edge and moved the roti off the heat. By then I was in a hurry, as the roti began to singe and there was another one I needed to turn on the flat pan. Meanwhile, Mom was steady and unruffled.

My favorite childhood bread was not roti, though; it was luchi—deep fried and puffy, warm and fresh, and simply amazing when rolled up with sugar. Because luchi was fried and not as healthy, Mom made it infrequently and even then only after modifying the recipe to half wheat and half white flour from its traditional use of all white flour. It made it a little healthier and the texture slightly firmer. Making luchi meant using a slotted spoon to twirl the bread a bit in the hot oil. Flicking your wrist accomplished this swirl and ensured the bread puffed completely, dramatically, and that it was flaky and stretched. When a luchi relaxed back into itself after it was taken off the heat, it was soft and tender.

Since I was born female I noted that it was the women who made these breads. The fact was that roti and luchi tasted best when hot, so someone needed to do the cooking while the others sat and ate. My brother never moved an inch toward the stove and my mother never suggested that he do so. He sat as grandly as my father at the table, waiting.

It seemed incredible to me. My father, yes, I could see. But my brother? This needed a revolution. But cooking luchi was firmly entrenched and there was a hierarchy even among the females.

I saw that pattern on a teenage trip to India when my cousin-sister, Indrani, and I giggled over makeup in her room. While I showed her my Max Factor lipgloss, mascara, and eye shadow, I noted that in the kitchen the family daughter-in-law was rolling breads by herself. It seemed normal for the household and though I felt slightly uncomfortable I remained seated at the vanity, occasionally seeing a wrist or palm shaping breads in the mirror's reflection. At home I would be helping. This would be the time to talk over the day. Indrani, fascinated by my meager collection of tubes and pots, didn't glance up. Indrani's vanity had three mirrors, hinged and scalloped at the top, creating what I called the princess effect. I could see a tiny bit of the kitchen in the upper left corner and, periodically, flat bread would be slapped down on the concrete counter. The kitchen was silent except for the slight sounds of roti being rolled and lined up to cook.

I ended up handing the makeup over. It was before India allowed many imports of Western goods and these things were rare for Indrani. This was one area in which I had an advantage. At the family tailor earlier, we had picked up some blouses and slips for my aunt. Indrani had watched me closely and said that it must be "so nice" shopping for my straight and mannish Western clothes as "there were so few pieces." She had seemed quite happy with all the decisions to be made about the blouse style, how the sleeves should be set, and the directions for the fall of the sari, though. Now, the coveted makeup seemed to make us square in girl points.

In Kansas, my girlhood eyes saw that the person making hot breads was always my mother. Indignant for her, I said this wasn't fair. My mother only smiled. I know now, forty years later, there is something satisfying in feeding those you love. Though getting a hot luchi for yourself should be one of life's pleasures, even for the cook.

ROTI (NONLEAVENED WHOLE WHEAT BREAD)

Makes 10 roti

2 cups fine whole wheat flour (*ata* or "chapati flour" found in Indian groceries)
½ cup water (approximately)
1 flat pan, preferably cast iron
1 metal rack that can sit over the burner

Put the flour (sifted grocery store wheat flour also works) in a large bowl and slowly add about ½ cup of water to form a soft dough. Knead the dough on a hard surface until it is smooth (about 8 minutes). Put the dough ball back into the bowl and cover it with a damp cloth for ½ hour.

Heat a flat cast-iron pan on the stove over medium heat. When it gets hot, turn the heat down to low. Keep another burner ready with a metal rack over the top (a latticework metal rack common for cooling cookies works for this). This burner will be used to "puff" the rotis.

Knead the dough again and divide it into 1½-inch balls. You might need to rub a little flour on your hands if the dough is sticky.

Flour a clean, hard surface and flatten one of the small dough balls into a patty. Roll this out, dusting with flour as needed, until the ball reaches about 5–6 inches in diameter. Pick up the rolled roti and place it onto the heated cast-iron pan. Let it cook for about 1 minute. Flip it with tongs or carefully with your fingertips and cook for about 30 seconds. Next, take the roti off the pan and place it directly on the metal rack over the second burner. The intense heat will make it puff up in seconds. Turn it over and let it sit on the heat for a few seconds. Place the puffed roti on a plate and cover with a cloth to keep warm. Best served warm; however, rotis are easily frozen in stacks wrapped in foil, or refrigerated for later meals. Reheat in hot 400°F oven.

SIPRA'S LUCHI (PUFFY FRIED BREAD)

Makes 8 small breads

½ cup wheat flour
½ cup white flour
½ teaspoon salt
2 tablespoons vegetable oil plus oil for frying
3½ fluid ounces water

Luchis puff up like balls and are best eaten hot. Use a deep frying pan or a small wok and a slotted spoon. First, mix the flours and salt in a medium-sized bowl. Add the 2 tablespoons oil and mix with your fingers until the mixture resembles bread crumbs. Slowly add the water to form a stiff ball of dough. Next, knead the dough ball on a clean surface for 10–12 minutes or until it is smooth. Place into the bowl and cover for 20–30 minutes. Knead the dough again and divide it into 12 equal balls. Keep the balls covered until they are rolled. Take one ball and roll it to about a 5½-inch round. Lay it aside and cover with plastic wrap. Roll each ball in this way, keeping them in a single layer under the plastic wrap.

Place paper towels over a platter and set aside. Heat about 1 inch of vegetable oil over medium flame in a small deep frying pan. Once it is very hot, gently lay one luchi into the hot oil, taking care not to splash. It should rise to the top of the oil and begin to sizzle. Using the back of a slotted spoon, rotate the luchi with small, quick swirls. The luchi will immediately puff up into a round ball. Continue to cook for 20 seconds, then turn the luchi over and cook for another 30 seconds. The luchi should be golden in color, not too brown. Remove from the oil with the slotted spoon and allow to drip for a moment before placing on the paper towel. Do not cover. Fry all the luchis in this manner and serve hot.

ALOO POROTA (POTATO-STUFFED WHEAT BREAD)

Makes 6 breads

½ cup wheat flour
½ cup white flour plus 2 tablespoons
pinch salt
5 tablespoons vegetable oil or ghee, approximately
½ cup water

Filling:
3 medium potatoes, boiled, peeled, and mashed (about 1½ cups mashed)
2 tablespoons cilantro, finely chopped
1 teaspoon fresh green chili, chopped (to taste)
½ teaspoon cumin powder
½ teaspoon salt (to taste)

Mix flour, water, and salt in a food processor for about 2 minutes until the ingredients come together in a dough ball. Add a few drops of water if the dough is too dry. Remove from the food processor and knead on a clean surface for 1–2 minutes. Set aside.

Add cilantro, green chili, cumin powder, and salt to the mashed potatoes and knead until well mixed. Taste the potato mixture to check spice and salt level.

Make 6 equal balls from the dough ball, and 6 equal balls from the potato mixture. Set aside. Take one dough ball, roll it in a little flour, and use a rolling pin to spread to about a 5-inch round. Place one potato ball in the circle and lift the sides of the dough to make a pouch or dumpling. Pinch the edges together at the top and flatten slightly. Do this for all 6 dough and potato balls. Set aside for 2 minutes. Then, roll each ball one at a time in flour and use a rolling pin to roll out into 7- or 8-inch porotas.

Place a porota on a hot, flat griddle and let it cook about 30 seconds. It should start to brown. Turn. Add about ½ teaspoon oil to the cooked side and spread evenly over the surface. The second side should cook about 30 seconds until it begins to brown. Turn. Add ½ teaspoon oil to the surface and spread it to the edges. Repeat. The porotas will be crispy and light brown with darker brown spots. Serve with tomato chutney and cool yogurt.

8

Grand Lake Menu for a Guru

I was eleven when the theology I had so wished for came to our house garbed in the saffron robes of a holy man. Mahananda Swami, a slightly built, bearded guru, emerged in front of 1403 S. Homer from a tan Buick LeSabre.

Swami pulled himself out of the rear seat by gripping the seat back and sliding forward to get leverage. People in white saris or kurtas gathered around his door to help. Mr. Towner next door slowed his steps behind his mower to watch, his weedless lawn barely needing its shave. Otherwise no one seemed to notice, which surprised me since I was waiting to be embarrassed. The local college marching band practiced in a nearby field and a tuba sounded a *blat* just as the guru stood. The band *oompah*-ed while he walked slowly toward our door.

Earlier, my parents had whispered a bit about what the neighbors might think and Baba made what he thought of as a "flustered-woman" noise.

"We'll get so close to God it won't matter," he said, fluttering his fingers toward the neighbor's house. Mom muttered as she walked by but with a chuckle in her voice, "*Baap re baap, shunaches?*" (Are you listening to this?). Baba clutched his chest in mock heart pain. "I may die tomorrow," he said, sneaking a look toward my mother.

Indians gathered from Kansas City, Joplin, and Tulsa, dressing in cotton rather than silk as an outward show of inner humbleness. When the clothes were subdued, so were the colors of the foods, I noticed. Mom made dal, cauliflower and potatoes, and *chole*: all golden in color. The table seemed to quietly pulse with turmeric, and the golden hue enveloped the kitchen. Some women wore the traditional saffron orange and their cotton saris were crisp. The color somehow did not seem bright, but toned like skin and the earth itself.

Because I was eleven and the women were busy, I did not get involved in the preparations for the Great Man. But I managed to peek. There was much talk about what types of food a guru would eat.

"Plain, plain," my mother said over the phone to a friend. "Simple vegetables only," and she nodded her head into the phone.

Her voice took on an Indian cadence when it was time for religious events, when there were more Indians about than usual, when there was a "proper" way to handle foods. Baba talked about the Great Man coming and looked skyward. It seemed to me he was rolling his eyes and then, from behind the paper he was reading in the living room, he began making the flustered noises.

"Uuuuuhh," and the paper rustled with the movement of his fingers.

At four o'clock, my mother sat in her gold velour recliner with a cup of hot tea and closed her eyes. Her eyelids pulsed a bit even after she sighed and settled into the chair. I had seen these signs before, so I retreated awhile. Eventually the kitchen filled up with uncles and aunties, all of them friends—not relatives—of my parents, everyone padding around in socks, and I passed between them unnoticed, sliding a bit on the linoleum to avoid collisions.

Later, sheets were laid down in the hallway to create a "pure" environment, and the guru, in orange robes and a long, graying beard, walked into the house and into my brother's room to rest. He held the saffron fabric that hung to his ankles away from his feet so he would not trip and the fabric pulled over his kneecap. But something was not right with the guru. His knees seemed weak, the caps bony, poking inward, though he was not pigeon toed. He was crowded by those walking alongside and just behind him in our narrow hall. He was perhaps trying to take narrower steps. But I squinted harder to get a bead on him and sure enough, he was knock-kneed. I had never seen a man walk like this. It seemed important. It was not a factor for the adults, though, this vulnerable walk. The men's voices softened. They waited to see if he might speak. The women tittered.

Mom made homemade cheese, chhana, for Swami, cut it into cubes, and sprinkled it with sugar. I imagined people went overboard making foods for a visitor like this, but vegetables, fresh juice, and cheese suited him and he ate it all. In my brother's room down the hall, he didn't have to eat in front of an audience.

This maneuver didn't defeat me, however, and I managed to peer furtively around the door. There was a flat folded blanket over which an orange cloth had been spread on the floor. The guru was perched on top of these, amid several small pillows. He ate in a methodical, traditional way. Fingers wrapped tidily around a piece of fruit, which was then placed between his lips. It seemed paced, rhythmic, at odds with pleasure, more like a requirement. Someone had hand-painted a red paisley design on white paper for him, and it hung on the wall behind his head. His hand, moving in front of the red dots, quivered and pulsed. Ever since fifth-grade science, I had thought of this traditional design for happiness and peace as a paramecium, and it distracted me. Then, I noted something more ominous: my brother's model airplane, hanging at an angle from the ceiling to simulate a jet in flight, moved a little on its strings. It must have been due to a slight stirring of air from the people moving around bringing in food, but I was sure the plane was about to crash into the teacher's chest. The idea of a chhana landing appalled me enough that I looked directly into the guru's eyes, which had found me at the door. I squeaked and fell back into the hall.

A little later, my mother emerged from the room with a small smile on her face. She indicated to a friend the empty plate she held and said quietly that the guru was finished "taking his food." The hall sheets were straightened a bit and Swami's door opened. He knock-kneed into the living room without incident and quietly sat on floor cushions that appeared for the event. Mom had seen him once, from rows and rows back under an open-sided tent, in Kolkata. His head had appeared as a small dot to her then. He gave food to the poor there and gave clothing to hundreds out of his ashram in Deoghar. His organization had disciples throughout the United States, too, and one nearby family had brought him through Kansas. Now, there was no getting around the fact that he sat in our living room, his head the normal size.

I felt the hope pulsing through the house. He would surely give a lecture. He would show us that nothing was fair and good alone. But he only nodded and smiled as people asked him how his trip was going, and as he asked them about the weather. All weekend, people spoke softly to Mahananda. They inclined their heads with polite inquiry. They nodded their heads sideways and said "*ji*" (yes) to what he said. I wanted to know about the cow thing, but no one was getting specific. All my life, no one had ever gotten specific about religious questions. Mostly, I ignored my need to know, but this man seemed like he could get to the bottom of things. I caught sight of my father at the front of the crowd, leaning toward the teacher, listening intently. He sat cross legged with his hands tucked under his knees. This time, it was my mother who rolled her eyes after catching sight of him.

It came out after a few hours that Mahananda did not want to lecture but to ride in our ski boat. Our boat was a green Newman with an 85-horsepower Evinrude motor, and I understood why he wanted to ride in it: on it, wind blew back your hair and the spray of water cooled your face. On it, we sometimes stopped and anchored with the waves laving the sides, and all around us were echoes of past summers spent in our cove of Grand Lake in Oklahoma, a little over an hour's drive from Pittsburg. Out in the middle, the water was almost always warm on top but your legs dangled into cool currents that induced a delicious shudder and thoughts about what might swim by in the dark sixty-mile-long lake. Its official name, Grand Lake O' the Cherokees, meant that all that water covered Indian burial grounds, forever swamping cultural sacred soil. Just when I could not take the idea of something brushing my legs anymore, we would start up the motor and ski. My brother and I skied for hours, making my father swirl the water with our circles in the cove, crossing the wake with little jumps, leaning over our slalom ski to touch the water at thirty, forty miles an hour.

Swamiji would not ski, not with those knees, but he wanted to taste the spray. I thought about Palmer and Pryor Resort, three miles outside of Grove, Oklahoma, and the barbecues held most weekends there. I visualized the boys and girls riding their motorized dirt bikes and the fishermen squishing by in their rubber mud boots with their pants tucked inside. "Mahananda Goes to Grand Lake" seemed like a sitcom. As we drove the hour and fifteen minutes it took to get from our house to the lake, I wondered whether the neighbors would do a fish fry this time or grill steaks. What would the slight and wiry Swami think of the large men with their affable language as they bellied up to the barbecue? Their teeth would flash around bites of meat while their gullets filled with beer. In Grove, amid all the swim trunks and wet tennis shoes, a man swathed in yards of saffron cotton, leather chappals on his feet, would be rare.

The gravel crunched a bit under the car tires when we turned in at the sign for Palmer and Pryor, and since I was nauseated from motion sickness, I cracked the window as soon as we slowed down. I liked the approach to the three rows of summer trailers and small homes. One row was up high, along the ridge. The next row was just behind the lakefront lots and was always quiet, as if the people who owned those spots didn't come very often. Our row was right near the swimming area. I was always either in the water or facing the water, where I could see our deck clearly between mulberry trees. Baba took the front road that day in order to show our guest the view.

As we pulled around, two minibikes gunned down the hill toward our car and at the last minute the waving drivers swerved around and passed by. Swamiji had been silent the entire trip and the noise seemed louder than usual. He seemed tickled by the exuberant bikers. He alighted, holding his saffron cloth in a fist to free his legs, and a group of us went to get the boat from its perch on the hill.

After hooking up the boat trailer out of sight of the others, Baba backed the trailer to the ramp, realigned at my frantic waving, and reversed until the trailer hubcaps were submerged. Tension gripped all of us as this went on—backing the trailer into the water could look so slick sometimes, but then there were the times it took six or seven tries and we were revealed as amateurs. After the hubcaps were successfully submerged, I climbed into the boat while my brother held the lead rope and Baba pulled the boat trailer out of the way, water pouring off its padded supports. After pulling the boat to the loading dock, Baba started up the engine, did a fancy swoosh, and slowly pulled around the stone point to the wooden dock in front.

The holy man's knuckles turned pale as he gripped my father's shoulder to step into the boat. We pulled slowly away from the dock and the boat was soon clipping along the waves. Swami held his seat with one hand and gripped the dash with the other. Baba sat on the top of the driver's seat. This put his face right in the wind, above the windshield, where the spray periodically flew up. Seeing this, Swamiji slid onto his own seat top.

"No!" Baba said, his voice a loud bark over the engine, his fingers shaking back and forth. "No, no, no, no."

As my father pictured a flying Swami tumbling into the waves, his voice rose with each "no." This was no hushed request. Baba could see long orange cotton tangling in Swami's legs and pulling him under the green water.

Distracted with these horrible thoughts, he jerked the steering wheel even though there was nothing to hit in the open water. Abruptly, Swamiji was airborne for just a moment and I, too, had visions of orange fabric twisting about under the waves. The world flipped in my vision. Suddenly, I saw Swami as a feather in the sky, robes and beard gently fluttering without volition, falling, falling. But Swami landed back in the seat, striking the leather with a slap. And because he wore smooth, soft cotton, he then slid forward until his knees struck the dash.

"Sit down," Baba said as he waved toward the floor. But Swami had already made his impact and now sat gazing up at my father, who was still tall in the seat with his head in the wind. I turned to see my mother shaking her head, her hand covering her eyes.

Swami's draped homespun cloth was not good for boating, while lake clothes—Baba's plain twill pants, my bare legs sticking to the hot vinyl seat under my shorts—held a firm grip here. The ashrams in India had no vinyl. Swami's world comprised wooden benches, cushions on bare floors, a mat. There, he folded his knees under himself and sat erect while meditating or while lecturing to gathered crowds. He sat thus, firm and still with no slipping, for hours.

The recipe for the chhana mentioned in this chapter is on page 13.

CHOLAR DAL (LENTILS)

Serves 6

1 cup cholar dal (chana lentils found in Asian/Indian stores are the
 best, or use small yellow spilt peas)
1 inch fresh ginger, grated
½ teaspoon turmeric
1 teaspoon salt (or more to taste)
1 whole dried red chili

2 tablespoons butter or clarified butter (ghee) or vegetable oil
1 bay leaf
1 teaspoon cumin seeds
½ teaspoon cayenne pepper (or to taste)
½ cup cauliflower pieces, browned slightly in oil (optional)

Wash lentils thoroughly. Fill a heavy saucepan ¾ full (with about 2 pints) of water, add lentils, cover, and boil, scooping foam from surface as needed. Add ginger, turmeric, and salt. Continue to cook at a hard simmer until the lentils are soft (about 1 hour). In a small pan, heat the ghee or vegetable oil and add the dried red chili, cumin seeds, and bay leaf. Stir-fry for 3 minutes or so. Put in the cayenne pepper and immediately pour the ghee mixture into the dal. Stir to mix. Gently simmer for an additional 5 minutes. Optional: In a small saucepan, stir-fry small pieces of cauliflower until slightly brown and crispy in vegetable oil or clarified butter (ghee). Add to dal at the very end and serve with rice.

ALOO COPI (CAULIFLOWER AND POTATOES)

Serves 6

2 medium potatoes, boiled and cooled in their jackets (can be done the day before and refrigerated)
1 medium cauliflower head
4 tablespoons oil
1 teaspoon whole cumin seeds
1 teaspoon ground cumin seeds
½ teaspoon ground coriander (optional)
¼–½ teaspoon turmeric
½ teaspoon cayenne pepper
½ fresh hot green chili, very finely chopped (optional)
1 teaspoon salt

Peel the boiled and cooled potatoes and cut them into ½-inch cubes. Break up the cauliflower into pieces about 1 inch across, soak in a bowl of water for 30 minutes or so, and drain. Heat the oil in a large frying pan. When hot, put in the whole cumin seeds. Let the seeds sizzle for a few seconds and then put in the cauliflower and stir-fry until the cauliflower pieces brown in spots, about 2–3 minutes. Cover, turn heat to low, and simmer for 5 minutes. Cauliflower should still be slightly crisp. Put in the potatoes, ground cumin, coriander, turmeric, cayenne, green chili, and salt. Stir gently to mix and continue to cook uncovered on low until the potatoes are heated through.

CHOLE (CHICKPEA CURRY)

Serves 4

- (2) 16-ounce cans chickpeas, drained and rinsed (or, soak equivalent dried chickpeas overnight, then simmer for 2 hours until tender, and strain)
- 5 tablespoons vegetable oil
- 2 medium onions, finely chopped
- 2½ teaspoons salt
- 1 fresh hot green chili, finely chopped
- 1 tablespoon fresh ginger, grated
- 4 tablespoons lemon juice
- ½ pound tomatoes, finely chopped, or (1) 16-ounce can chopped tomatoes
- 1 tablespoon ground coriander
- 1 tablespoon ground cumin
- ½ teaspoon ground turmeric
- ¼ teaspoon cayenne pepper (or to taste)
- ½–1 cup water
- 1 teaspoon garam masala (optional)

Drain and rinse chickpeas and set aside. Or, use soaked chickpeas that have been simmered over low heat for 2 hours until tender. In a small bowl, mix the salt, green chili, ginger, and lemon juice and set aside. Heat the oil in a heavy stockpot. When hot, add onions and stir-fry until they just begin to brown. Add chickpeas, tomatoes, coriander, cumin, turmeric, and cayenne. Mix well. Reduce heat and simmer for 15 minutes. Add water and continue to simmer another 10 minutes. Add lemon juice/spice mixture to the chole and mix. Add garam masala if desired. Serve with Indian bread or rice.

9

An Indian Kitchen in Kansas

Though issues of theology, even before Swami's visit, always teased at the edges of my mind, by second grade, I was often in a world of fantasy. I knew what reality was, sure, but I preferred daydreams: pleasant ones about flying a one-girl aircraft I called a hover around the neighborhood. I'd kick the dirt and scuff the grass on the way home, but my thoughts were not earthbound.

My childhood home was a ranch-style yellow clapboard with a band of light red brick about three feet high across the front. It sat about five blocks from my grade school in the middle of the block among other such houses, some blue clapboard, some red brick, and it was right next to Morris and Mabel's place. Walking home, I was lost in my hover vision, coasting around with my friends, flying free over the fields behind our house, but I sensed Morris, whom I considered my American grandfather, sitting conspicuously in his green mesh folding chair outside his side door at 3:15. He always timed it so.

In India, a grandfather was a serious responsibility. You listened well to a grandfather. You gave him respect and brought him sweets should there be any in the kitchen. So even though I was more interested in an after-school snack for myself, I came back to earth from my daydream and walked over.

"What's going on today?" Morris called, dropping the newspaper he was reading onto his lap.

I went the twenty or so steps to his porch and plopped down. Morris wore baggy, pleated trousers with a thin black belt, a soft plaid button-up short-sleeve cotton shirt, and black loafers. His bristling gray eyebrows tufted above blue eyes and black-rimmed glasses.

I liked it best when we sat outside. There was always a car to watch going by, the college band to hear in the nearby field, or robins to entertain us. I flopped on the porch and tossed my bag on the ground. I slouched. When we were inside, I hummed to myself between the times Morris spoke, and when he did I answered quickly. I sat straight in the armchair. I invariably began to compare the difference in the sizes of my thumbnails. I fidgeted and tried to figure out a way to say I had to go home without being rude. I decided somewhere along the way that because he and Mabel never had children, they didn't learn to speak very quickly, not having to keep up with a darting child passing through the kitchen or running over the porch on the way to a bike. I did not bring anything edifying to the conversation, but I had adopted Morris and he had adopted me, and so I visited. Even then I knew there was a whole world of experience he never mentioned. I think he knew about my daydreams.

In Mrs. Pistole's second grade, I spent hours of class gazing out of the window. I perfected a stare trained on the teacher, but fuzzy, so the sky was clear and foremost in my mind. I stayed in my inner vision until someone pulled me out. When the teacher called on me, my eyes sharpened, another side of my brain kicked in, and I answered correctly every time. I won a giant chocolate bar because I answered all the math questions first. I shared the bar with the class and went back to thinking about clouds. I kept up pretty well for someone thinking two sets of thoughts and, mostly, no one noticed.

Clouds were important because in my daydream I usually piloted a bright yellow hover and the yellow looked so vibrant against blue fluff. Sometimes I chose the red or royal blue hover models from the garage. My friends and I flew around in them, even over the fields behind my house, and visited the spooky pond and old house with a junk pile around it in the darkly wooded back copse. I was an A student, but after a year of this I was getting Cs in spelling.

Third grade teacher Mrs. Phillips: "It is understandable why Nina is having trouble spelling in English, with your two languages at home."

My mother, turning her head slightly to me, narrowing her eyes: "Yes, we'll work on that."

It's safe to say my mother knew why I was deplorable in spelling: daydreaming and complete lack of studying. I stifled a giggle.

As I sat with Morris that day, a new thought occurred to me.

"I'm tired of being watched."

I had never said this to anyone before, hadn't really thought it through. All I knew was Mom always insisted that we dress well, look our best, behave well, in part because we represented India to the town. I was in grade school. I didn't want to represent India. It made me weary to stick out all the time.

Instead of answering, Morris told me about being a lawyer in Pittsburg during the McCarthy years. Mabel came out and showed me a grainy newspaper photo of herself with her hair swept up and pearls at her neck, Morris in a dark suit and bushy eyebrows, and others sitting at a table. The photo let me peek into another world of a younger Mabel and Morris, a fancy-dress, Disney-like world of relationship and talk where I sensed I had no place. It was a dinner, a sophisticated banquet with society and business people. Mabel held the clipping like there was something important about the picture and she pointed: *those two were Communists*. I nodded, like I knew something secret. She said the word and then closed the album before I could read the caption.

"Now that was being watched," Morris said.

I got the idea that this would suck the fun out of most parties.

There was a newspaper article about us in the *Pittsburg Headlight* on August 10, 1966, when I was still preschool age. The large half-page photo collage showed Mom with her hair done up and dressed in a silk sari with pearls around her neck while she worked on her master's thesis. In another photo, I stood next to her at the stove and while she stirred a pot, I stirred a smaller version on an unlit burner. The middle photo showed me on sturdy legs in front of my child-sized kitchenette. I am cooking something while talking on a plastic phone and looking directly into the camera. My brother is earnestly playing with G.I. Joes. The headline read "Indian Family Adapts Readily to U.S. Culture," and the captions read "American Toys are Tops," "Old World New World," and "Works for Masters Degree." Mom was "that rare combination of woman, a really intelligent, humorous, beautiful being who keeps up with the world, has opinions, yet manages to be calm, gracious, soft-spoken, a woman who is superbly feminine."

But what I knew about her came out of the kitchen. It was the place in our house where I never daydreamed. I was always solidly there, among swirling aromas and heat and popping onions. In my late afternoon visit to Morris, I did not eat a snack even though Mabel wore an apron over one of her flowered housedresses with large buttons fastening the front. She did not hover over the stove or rummage in the refrigerator for something to bring out. When my stomach growled, I knew where to go. Within seconds, I was up and heading for Mom's kitchen.

The article in the *Pittsburg Headlight* had quoted my mother as saying she could find most things in our small-town grocery that she needed for Indian cooking. She was being gracious. As she walked down the aisles at the grocery store on Broadway, Mom passed canned beans, Uncle Ben's rice in small red boxes, macaroni and cheese, Velveeta, tuna cans, and Cap'n Crunch cereal. She did not pass fresh plain yogurt, which to her was a staple for many Indian dishes. Nor did she see fresh eggplant, gourd, or most of the spices needed for our foods: cardamom, ginger, cumin seeds, coriander powder, and dried red chili, to name a few. Lentils, other than standard split peas, were not available. She began adding half a tomato to curries in place of plain yogurt at the end of the cooking process to balance the flavors. She always had on hand whatever fresh vegetable was in season and she alternated between recipes for American pot roasts, pork chops, and rice and dal. The proof was in the pudding, so to speak, of my two culinary homelands.

Mom's refrigerator was stocked with condiments for burgers or sandwiches, with milk and eggs, leftover Hamburger Helper, shrimp or egg curry, and sometimes tomato chutney. The shrimp curry, especially the second day, was always my favorite. But oh, the lightness of egg curry with the spices infiltrating the eggs—it was never heavy like a meat curry, but succulent just the same. I learned to roll the hard-boiled eggs in hot oil until the skin blistered a little and turned golden all over. I then pierced them with a knife before letting them rest gently in the curry alongside long strips of onions and chunks of potato, alongside ginger and cinnamon and cloves, alongside savory bay and garlic and cayenne. When we made this curry, there were often no leftovers.

Maraschino cherries almost always bobbed in Mom's refrigerator, too. That Saturday, I stood at the refrigerator door looking intently at the shelves, trying to avoid a conversation about yard work. The mix of food made it clear:

I did not have to choose one homeland over another. I did not immediately pick egg curry, or even shrimp.

I stared at the maraschino cherries while my father talked about grass. Our neighbors, the Towners to the south and Morris and Mabel to the north, had tidy, well-clipped lawns. The Towners' grass, especially, seemed more uniform, darkly green and cut in a pattern that turned the blades in unison to the sun. Our lawn had issues with renegade clover and dandelions and Mom tried to make up for it with bright marigolds and red petunias. It mostly worked.

"Oh *ma go*. I don't feel so good," Baba said. I glanced over my shoulder. He made no eye contact with anyone.

That day the peach English rose on the south side of the house was taken down, and Mom had just walked into the kitchen where Baba was washing his hands.

Clipping the grass was my dad's job and he felt it was his God-given right to mow in straight lines. There had been an amazing red rose that climbed up an oriental-style trellis on the north side of the house. One day it was there, adding a dashing bit of color to the front yard, and the next it was gone, done in by the mower. Mom periodically came in during the warm months with bursts of news of other ornamental plants that were obliterated in the drive to mow. Mom looked grim as she thought of the peach English rose, its branches in a fray, unsalvageable.

Baba clutched his chest.

My brother guffawed at his place at the table.

Baba's face contorted.

"*Uff*," Mom waved him away.

"I may die tomorrow."

She rolled her eyes. The peach rose had not been in a flowerbed but out in the open grass, taunting the mower. While my mother muttered about people who tracked in dirt, having given up on getting satisfaction on the rose bush, and my father continued to lament his health, I refocused on the refrigerator door, considering the cherries.

There is no equivalent to a maraschino cherry in Indian food. There's pickled lime—that sour-hot relish that bites the tongue that all adult Indians inexplicably like—or pickled sweet mango. There's *jillipea*, but it's more like a fried fritter soaked in syrup. It *is* orange, an odd color, really, for a dessert, like red dye #40 is an odd color radiating out of the maraschino cherry bottle in the refrigerator door. But there's a bit of a soggy crunch when you bite into jillipea, and it's not trapped in a jar—it's made fresh, a delicious and very sweet treat that is especially good at outdoor fairs or from the carts of street vendors.

The cherry jar was there as usual. I opened the lid and carefully dipped in my spoon, taking care to avoid the thin islands of crystallized sugar on top, trapped a cherry on the side of the glass, and dragged it up and into my mouth. It never met expectations. The scent the jar released was not the sort of smell I was drawn to even at twelve. An intriguing kind of smell to me was woody and scented with ferns and the fronds of innumerable other plants, not chemical. I wouldn't have chosen maraschino red, either, but red like henna, like mothering.

But I raided the cherries. They were so cheerfully bright, and amnesia would set in about their taste. I closed the door, leaving a collection of slick cherries bobbing, and knew that my mother had thought of me at the IGA. She had walked along the aisle, her bangles chiming along with the clacking of the cart, and had reached up above her shoulder to get the small red jar with its white label and green border. Neither of my parents ate maraschino cherries.

The jar, sitting oddly translucent in the door, was there for me.

JILLIPEA (FRITTER IN SYRUP)

½ cup flour
2 teaspoons dry yeast
2 teaspoons buttermilk or 1 teaspoon yogurt
½–1 cup vegetable oil

Syrup:
2 cups sugar to 1 cup water
a few drops yellow or orange food coloring
a few cardamom seeds, if desired

Mix the flour, yeast, and buttermilk and set aside for 20–25 minutes. In the meantime, mix the syrup and set aside. Heat the oil in a heavy pan or wok. When hot, fill an icing press or snip the end of a honey container and fill with the jillipea batter. Squeeze in a crazy pattern into the hot oil. After the strings of jillipea batter get crispy and light brown, remove from the oil with a slotted spoon and drain on a paper towel. When the jillipea is dry and no longer soft, place in the syrup for 1 minute. Remove and eat.

TOMATO CHATNI (TOMATO CHUTNEY)

Serves 6–8

1½ tablespoons vegetable oil
1 teaspoon black mustard seeds
5–6 tomatoes, cut into chunks
¾ cup sugar
¼ cup raisins
1 tablespoon lemon juice, or more to taste

Heat oil in a saucepan. When hot, add mustard seeds and let sizzle for 20 seconds. Add tomato pieces and fry for 2 minutes. Reduce temperature to medium-low and simmer for about 10 minutes. Add sugar and mix well. Continue to simmer gently for another 10 minutes. Add raisins and continue to simmer another 10 minutes, until the chutney begins to thicken. Take pan off heat and add lemon juice. Serve at room temperature or chilled.

CHINGRI MAACH MALAI CURRY (SHRIMP CURRY COOKED IN COCONUT MILK)

Serves 8

2 tablespoons vegetable oil
1 bay leaf
4–5 whole cloves
1 piece cinnamon stick, 1½ inches long

4–5 cardamom pods
1 onion, cut in half lengthwise and then very finely sliced
1 teaspoon cumin powder
1 teaspoon coriander powder
½–1 teaspoon turmeric powder
½ teaspoon cayenne powder (or to taste)
2 pounds shrimp, peeled and deveined
(1) 14-ounce can coconut milk
¼ cup raisins
½ cup peas
1 teaspoon salt (or to taste)
½ teaspoon sugar
1 inch fresh ginger, grated, or ½ teaspoon ginger powder
garam masala (optional)

Heat oil in a heavy pot and add bay leaf, cloves, cinnamon, and cardamom. Let the whole spices sizzle for 10 seconds. Add sliced onions and fry until light brown. Drain excess oil. Add cumin, coriander, turmeric, cayenne, and a small amount of water to keep mixture from burning. Cover and simmer for 5 minutes. Add shrimp and peas and stir. Cover and cook for 3–4 minutes. Add coconut milk, raisins, salt, sugar, and ginger. Simmer until heated through. Sprinkle with garam masala if desired and serve.

DIMAER DALNA (EGG CURRY)

Serves 6–8

8 eggs, hard boiled and peeled
1 cup vegetable oil

2 tablespoons vegetable oil
1 bay leaf
4–5 whole cloves
1 piece cinnamon stick, 1½ inches long

4–5 cardamom pods

2 onions, cut in half lengthwise and then very finely sliced

2 medium potatoes, boiled in their jackets and cooled

1 inch fresh ginger, grated, or 1 teaspoon ginger powder

½ teaspoon cayenne (or to taste)

½ teaspoon turmeric powder

1–2 teaspoons salt

½ tomato, cut into 2 pieces, or 2 tablespoons plain yogurt

water

In a small saucepan with high sides, or a small wok, add 1 cup oil and heat. When hot, carefully lower a hard-boiled egg into the oil with a slotted spoon. The oil will sputter a little. Brown the egg and turn it with the spoon. Once all sides are evenly brown, lift the egg out of the oil, letting some of the oil drip back into the pan, and set aside on a paper towel while you brown the rest of the eggs.

Heat 2 tablespoons oil in a heavy pot and add bay leaf, cloves, cinnamon, and cardamom. Let the whole spices sizzle for 30 seconds. Add sliced onions and fry until the onions just start to turn brown. Peel the cooled potatoes and cut into 2-inch chunks. Add potato cubes to the onion mixture. Add the ginger, cayenne, turmeric, salt, and tomato pieces or yogurt. Mix well, add enough water to just reach the tops of the potatoes, turn the burner to medium-low, and simmer for 15 minutes.

Gently pierce each of the eggs once with a sharp knife to let the flavors of the curry inside. Add the browned eggs to the onions and potatoes. Heat through and serve with rice.

10

Attic Fans and Flying Typewriters

This is what changed the food I ate for dinner: a boy slid a window up in language arts class and threw out a typewriter. It was during the fourth quarter of my seventh-grade year. The row of six-by-three-foot wood-framed windows that lined the outside walls of our school had iron pulls along the bottom and a latch lock halfway up on the cross trim. It was easy to flip the latch and push these windows up, unlike the hermetically sealed windows in the new school, which was built in time for me to graduate. The typewriter fell two stories and crashed onto the grass.

The next day was worse. The day after the flying typewriter incident, the class, both lawless and occasionally sheepish, shuffled in line as they went into Room 303. Something of the criminal element crept into me as well as I folded forbidden chewing gum into my mouth just outside the door. There was an unspoken mischievous current running through the group of boys and girls with tidy hair and tucked-in shirts, and in reaction we shifted from foot to foot, banged our books against our thighs, and laughed loudly in the hall.

Once inside the room, a boy bumped my desk with his chair as he hopped it forward into the aisle. I looked back and saw pencils flying through the air and heard shouts of "hey man" called across the room. Then the teacher, Miss N—, stood up, and her chair almost tipped over as she pushed it back and walked around her desk, grabbing an aerosol can on the way. She pulled back her arm and flung the can hard. She wanted to hit the loudest boy just to get him to sit down, to answer her, to stop scraping his desk legs against the linoleum. She threw with her wrist bent, and with my softball experience I could have told her it wouldn't make the distance. She had poor upper body strength. The can made it only to the front row, not all the way to the back of the room like she hoped, and she hit my friend LuAnn on the lip and made her bleed. Miss N— then left the room for good.

After that, my mother, who had been a substitute teacher for a year or so, came to teach us language arts. Everything settled down at school. Within days, though, the foods in our refrigerator completely changed and I started making Hamburger Helper. It was not a stellar culinary era for our family.

The difference between my family's two cooking styles was partially a factor of time. Indian food took longer at the stove, and the typewriter incident changed Mom's schedule. She no longer had the energy to cook complicated meals during the week.

By then, Mom wore pantsuits to go along with her English teaching: no more saris outside the house. There was some admiring talk about how Mom could teach English even though it was her second language; I wanted to correct people and tell them that really, it was her third language after Bengali and Hindi. In class, she expected us to read and answer questions and take tests. It all seemed so clear. There was a little pencil tapping from the boys in the back, but after Mom rearranged our seats even that stopped. In line outside the classroom door, someone called me a teacher's pet, but only once and halfheartedly.

When I cooked our American hamburger-helped meals, I pulled the frying pan out of the oven drawer and put it on the largest burner of the chocolate-brown stove. Box-mix stroganoff required a small container of sour cream, and I mixed it into the browned meat, added the noodles and water and spice packet, and there was dinner. No one ever complained about having it weekly, but now I cannot bring myself to eat even a more authentic version of stroganoff, with thinly sliced steak, without a little shudder. I made the other box-mix varieties, too. I remember curly noodles and minced meat, dried potatoes and minced meat, noodles and tomato sauce and meat. After the bland stroganoff nights there was ice cream, or sometimes sweet carrot (*gajor*) *halwa*.

Halwa was a comfort food for my dad and mom, and I would always take a portion, though I didn't love it as they did. Mom made it quickly with carrots and pistachios and sweetened milk. It was lightly flavored with cardamom. Eating it was rewarded by proximity to the pleasurable sounds around the table, utensils clinking, my parents chatting, a feeling of being in the center of things.

The nights I cooked American food, the spice aromas were quiet, which pleased my father. Baba associated intense Indian aromas with excessive lawn ornaments in the front yard, or a bathtub used as a flowerpot on the porch. Strong aroma was somehow an unwanted clue to our "otherness" in a town filled with the scents of frying cheeseburgers, chicken, and pot roast with baked potatoes. Grilling onions and garlic would make him frown. Those smells were something for apartment dwellers in crowded cities, where the neighbors might complain to themselves about the family next door. He overheard such complaints as a college student in Chicago in the 1950s and felt it was low class to cook heavily scented food in the United States, though he would have thought the same in India. Spices upset his stomach, and food was not what he first wanted to smell when walking in the door.

But it was Saturday, and after the long school week my mother made meat curry and the entire house became fragrant. The onions browning in oil scented with cardamom, cloves, cinnamon, and bay filled the air and welcomed the rest of us home. She accompanied the *jhol* (wet) curry with potatoes coated in *posto* (crushed poppy seeds).

These dishes, however, spelled trouble—gale-force wind kind of trouble. As soon as my father came in from working in the yard, he made a beeline for the attic fan closet. It was a half-width door made of solid maple like the rest of the woodwork in the house. This door opened into a tiny hall that ended at my brother's room, and when you opened the skinny door you could not go through. The blockage felt scary somehow.

The attic fan, a contraption that seems to be obsolete these days, was rarely used in our house except for aroma eradication. The smell of cinnamon, cloves, bay, ginger, and onions did not linger at 1403 S. Homer. First, my father opened a window on the far side of the house. Then he flipped the switch to the fan, causing the machinery in the closet to rumble. The very walls shook. The fan in the hall ceiling would winch open and its great yawning maw would suck and spew, seemingly at the same time. The draft was impressive. The noise and wind to match lasted for a full ten minutes or until my father decided the smell was tolerable.

Sometimes this happened in the dead of winter. Shivering, we sat at the table until the air settled down. If I bent close to my plate, the guilty spices would still be wafting, quiet but sure. By the time I was a teen, I would start the attic fan myself, before Baba came home, in anticipation.

SHORTCUT GAJOR HALWA (SWEET CARROT CONFECTION)

Serves 4–6

1 pound carrots, grated
1 can sweetened condensed milk
1 tablespoon vegetable oil
½ cup raisins
¼ cup slivered almonds or pistachios, halved
⅛ teaspoon ground cardamom

Put the grated carrots in a heavy saucepan with enough condensed milk to barely cover. Cook over medium heat until the carrots begin to soften. Continue to stir to avoid burning and cook until the mixture is almost dry. Remove from heat. Put the oil in a large frying pan, add the carrot-milk mixture (halwa), and then add the raisins, nuts, and cardamom. Stir frequently until very soft. The halwa will be slightly moist in texture.

MANGSHO (AROMATIC LAMB CURRY WITH POTATOES)

Serves 6–8

8 tablespoons vegetable oil
1 large onion, finely chopped
½ to 1 green chili, finely chopped
6 cloves garlic, minced
2 pounds lamb (beef can be substituted), boned and cut into 1-inch cubes

2 tomatoes, chopped, or (1) 14-ounce can of tomatoes

1 tablespoon ground cumin

1 tablespoon ground coriander

½ teaspoon ground turmeric

¼–1 teaspoon cayenne pepper

2 teaspoons salt

1 pound medium potatoes, peeled and cut in chunks

2½ cups water

1 bunch cilantro, chopped, stems discarded

Heat the oil in a large, heavy stockpot over high heat. When hot, put in the onions and stir-fry until the onions begin to brown. Add the green chili and garlic. Put in the meat and stir-fry for 5 minutes. Put in the tomatoes, cumin, coriander, turmeric, cayenne pepper, and salt. Continue to cook on high heat for 10–15 minutes, stirring frequently. Add the potatoes and the water. Add the cilantro. Cover, leaving the lid slightly ajar, and cook on low heat for about 1 hour and 10 minutes (1½ hours for beef).

11

Mother Tongue

Bengali, my mother tongue, was something I took right out of the air only to give it away. My parents would speak, mumble, or laugh it out loud, unafraid of my stealth. Of course, my first efforts at speech were feeble, focused on food and comfort. No one worried. I then moved on to persuasion. "*Chan cor, dada, chan cor,*" I said, beseeching my brother to wash in the bath. This, too, was treated with gentle humor.

But it is said that what can be named with words is not real, merely a reflection of truth or what is called God. Each word is a trail of crumbs, evidence. Each word, a gift in proportion to the spirit in which it was uttered. Inside my head, Bengali made its noises. But even as I grasped for them, my Bengali tongue went still. I was down to one true fluency and American English had nothing to say about all the god stories in India. The food on my plate, too, was silent. The world sang its reality: birds, frogs, water, all singing, all wordless. Language became a fetter and at age five, school age, I had no word for sorrow.

Aromas and occasional visits by Indian gurus linked me to India, but otherwise, my family was essentially on its own. There were no other families nearby from Bengal or from other states in India with which to keep up traditions, speak our language, cook our food. Joplin, Missouri, had some. There were more in Tulsa, Oklahoma, and Kansas City. Periodically, we climbed into the Ford Elite with its long, pale yellow nose and drove along the flat wheat fields, with clusters of grain elevators visible long before reaching them and hamlets belly-up to the highway, to gather for puja or other dinners, where my parents seamlessly transitioned into their second world.

Or, that world came to us. The sensate theater of it all, the color, the aromas, the lovely silks and jewelry gripped me. A stilled moment flashes in my memory: I see a woman's face tip up and her throat work as she laughs; our living room lamp illuminates golden skin, white teeth, black hair, and a clutch of other women in vibrant colors. Behind them, my mother sits along the couch, and the lamplight slashes across her face. Something about her posture, her subtle straightness, a slight desolation in her eyes, sets her apart as she looks into the near distance, her profile breathtaking. I cannot take my eyes off her. I wait for her to drop her shoulder, to sharpen her gaze, but the tableau is frozen on her face and always the light hits her folded hands just so. Suddenly, a group of men walks in front of me and when I look again, Mom is turned away, the silk of her sari rustles with the movement of her body, and in her animation her face is no longer eternal.

During one of my parents' parties, groups of friends formed and re-formed, their language dipping and rising, their laughter ringing. As the food was arranged, aromas became pronounced. The good table was set, not in courses, but all at once. The art of eating was revealed by knowing which dishes to eat first, second, and with which to finish, not by how they were presented: a vegetable first, then dal with chutney alongside, then any chicken, fish, or meat, and perhaps a *raita* (yogurt) dish to finish and settle. Alongside language, my mother tongue attenuated to this organization of spices, flavors, and textures in the mouth.

As the food was served, the swell of language resembled a flutter of birdsong tumbling on the wind. Bengali is musical to those with an ear for it, my mother said. During that party I could hear what she meant: word inflections flirted up and down a scale, the English that sporadically thrust through sounding stretched, tonal, and midwestern.

English suddenly seemed hard edged, its phrases a staccato across the living room. It sounded something like "*amar* Dell Computer *kalkae aeshaechay*" when the men spoke about a computer that arrived yesterday, the rhythm of the two languages worlds apart. The women used English words for things like georgette and nylon and chocolate. But always for cooking, the phrases sang: *longca, labungo, ada, jeerae, dhonae, chini* (red chili, clove, ginger, cumin, coriander, sugar).

In India, language is a curiosity. First there are so many, plus hundreds of dialects. The existence of the field of linguistics itself is indebted to an Englishman in India. Sir William Jones, sent to India as a judge in 1783, taught himself Sanskrit and found ties to what he believed might be a parent Indo-European tongue. By then Sanskrit was a dead language, used only in ceremonial contexts by priests. These priests had been the bearers of Sanskrit for centuries, memorizing the ancient Vedas, or sacred hymns, and passing them on from one generation to the next. Jones noticed many striking similarities between Sanskrit and the newer European languages, suggesting a common historical source—the Indo-European mother tongue, so to speak.

Despite this common source, I was not proficient in Bengali, which meant I was effectively cut off from my family culture. By 1975, I witnessed my mother teaching English almost every day and I spoke English almost exclusively. At home my parents continued to have discussions in Bengali, which motivated me to understand all that they said, but sometime in my teens they stopped speaking to me in Bengali. I waited for the occasional time when Mom would say something to me in our family language, perhaps on a shopping excursion, when it was usually something she considered in bad taste to say in front of a sales clerk. Clothes hangers would be shifted casually and wide-collared shirts and corduroy skirts would drift under her fingers as she would say something like "The price is too high, let's wait for a sale." More often, it was just something like "It's time to go, Nin. I've got to get dinner going." I lived for those moments of being in the club. I remember the pang of my father speaking to me exclusively in English when I came home from college one weekend. I toyed with the idea of learning Hindi, offered then at the University of Missouri, but decided against it. After all, it was the ties to Bengal via Bengali I wanted, not the nationally recognized language of another Indian state.

There was no question that language skills went over well at the party. Even just a word or two helped, but with all the aunties and uncles watching, I struggled to come up with anything more than a stutter. My brother and I dressed up, though after all the hellos we did not figure much into the main social swirl. The women were dressed in rich hues of silk, and sandals slapped the back of their heels. Their black hair was swept up. Jewelry flashed. The men wore dark pants and white shirts, and their greetings included hearty laughs and shoulder slaps.

Our table was covered from side to side with steaming dishes of rice, chicken curry, *aloo copi*, and shrimp cutlet. Mom had been in a cooking mood, so chops lined a long glass dish as well. Women standing near the platters dazzled me in their colorful dress, as did the array of foods: red tomato chutney, snappy green beans, golden dal.

I swung my legs from the couch and watched the adults arrive. Shati-Auntie and P.K.-Uncle had come from Joplin. Shati and P.K.'s son, Shaun, who was much younger than me, was there, but otherwise there were no other children. Mom's seven-foot gold brocade couch was the best place to see the action. When I sat there, after a while the adults forgot to ask me questions about school or what I was eating or what my grades were, and they began to interact as if I were not there. P.K.-Uncle smiled and laughed his large laugh. Shati-Auntie and other women sat, their delicate golden-skinned fingers fluttering in the air, resting lightly in their laps, and in general following the rise and fall of their conversation. Their bangles chimed in sync with their voices. My father held court behind his leather-covered bar. His arms were strong and muscular; he had built the room himself. I remember him digging the foundation, balancing on the rooftop pounding shingles, and later, hanging the heavy six-by-six rough-cut beams of wood along the ceiling. This is a country where you can do it yourself, he said. No waiting for the carpenter-man or the concrete-man or the shingle-man to build what you want. No extra money needed to get the job you already paid for done when you want it done.

Now, he smiled and dropped ice into some Scotch for me to taste. I frowned and shook my head after one tiny sip and he was amused. Mom, who was making noises behind my back that meant she was not happy, relaxed her shoulders after I returned the glass to my dad. The ladies asked for Coke, usually, or Sprite. There were a lot of men popping lightly salted warm cashews into their mouths. I could smell the luscious aroma. Just before the party, Mom had lightly fried raw cashews and salted the rich nutmeat on beds of paper towels. I surreptitiously grabbed a handful as I began to make my rounds.

But when I walked up to a group of adults, everyone around me started speaking English. Smooth, musical Bengali, made by a relaxation around the chin and the tongue, turned into words with distinct, delineated lip movements.

"*Camon ah-ches?*" became "How are you?" The flow of dialogue changed and my uncles made self-conscious chuckling noises. Standing in front of the group, the ice clinked as I focused on the men's wrists jiggling their Scotch glasses. They dropped their chins a little and I heard them suck air between their teeth while they waited for me to answer their questions. Bengali words that seemed to roll smoothly—graceful in acknowledging respect for an elder, or sweet to mark indulgence for a young niece, for instance—turned into a flat midwestern greeting, devoid of any Indian cultural story. Because my Bengali was so bad and because I was shy about that, I spoke English, though in my head I recognized Bengali as my native language and I avidly followed all that was said around me.

I felt correct pronunciation was the ticket into the club of ease and elegant speech at those Indian functions. Not wanting to cause a halt to the conversations around the room, I ceased stopping at groups of adults and generally flitted by, smiling and continuing on as if I had somewhere to go. I learned early that voice—our personal, up-front bearer of inner thoughts—could divide as much as unite.

But once, I sang in Bengali. The scene was this: I sat forward in the back seat of my grandfather's car in the hill town of Ranchi. The car was black and the seats tan, broad, and deep. The steering wheel was the kind that seemed to span the width of your shoulders, with a large round medallion in the middle, meant for turning the car more easily without power steering. My grandfather rhymed in Bengali from the front seat. The housekeeper's son, Mukund, usually acted as a driver, but that day my dadu drove. Dadu was not a tall man, longer in the leg than the torso, and he had a beak nose. The effect from the outside of the car was disconcerting: his profile came just to the top of the steering wheel. His almost-bald head bobbed as he raised his right hand on the beat of the rhyme. He was heavy on the bass notes, so it was easy to follow as we went down the small roads between the houses and around the paddies of rice, singing: *Ami, Bangala boosta pari, kinto bolta pari na!* (I can understand Bengali, but I cannot speak it!). It seemed so funny to me since I was singing this in Bengali, and we carried on all the way to Main Road. After that, traffic was mixed, with rickshaws, people walking, loose animals, carts, and cars, so the game ended.

Dadu began to honk his horn and swerve around people. We continued at a crawl as the road became choked in the middle of town. Somehow, though, the throng parted and we rarely had to stop. Dadu began to mutter darkly about the pedestrians. He sometimes flung his arm wide to make a point. I am sure it was not so, but I got the feeling the crowd knew my dadu, and they moved in respect for Mr. Banerji, and out of fear of his car. In any case, the car parted the sea of people.

As a teenager, I felt correct pronunciation was the key to cultural identity. What rolled smoothly through my head did not translate into sounds coming out of my mouth. So, at fourteen, I asked my mother to teach me: I gathered pencils and paper, readied my mind, and sat at the kitchen table while she cleared dinner. I envisioned doing exercises like the English sentence diagrams in language arts class. But she didn't do it; this woman who made teaching her life's work became vague about something she needed to do and wandered off, thinking, I am sure, it was too late to untangle my tongue. It wasn't too late, I wanted to tell her. I still thought in Bengali as often as not, the English and Bengali intertwined, connected, part of me. But we never had our lesson, and my pronunciation remained abominable.

In direct fashion, language ties people together as strongly as food. Both involve a constant working of the mouth, both, the use of the tongue. Taking food into the body to live is incredibly intimate. So, too, is voice: the audible self.

When my extended family visits, in addition to Indian food, a spate of Bengali spreads throughout my home. Once family descends, the lilt and tone of my childhood language fills spaces English cannot. Perhaps because of this, I've been noticing how we talk—and the fact that much of it is done in our heads.

It is true that the effort to speak a common language creates a bond. I have seen toothless Greek women smile and wave and hand me baklava without being asked because I said *kali`mera*, good morning. I have listened while old Arab farmers in Tunisia fondly called my blond husband "son of Tunis" because of his smiling efforts at their mother tongue while we were in the Peace Corps. The native straw hat he wore with his grin helped, but it was his opening salvo, *shnuwwa walik, assla:ma* (hello, how are you?), and the subsequent conversation that really bridged the culture gap.

It's true, though, we can speak the same language and not understand. We cluster around the world of appearance. Our capacity to get beyond familiar separations is all that I call hope in the world.

Communication is a varied event in any case. There's body language, choice of dress, facial expression, and more. And no matter which part of the world you are from, forms of communication can interfere with the experience of food. The monks of old might have had the best idea living in silence and meditation. Many modern-day retreats offer a meditative, silent schedule as well as quiet meals, a time you are meant to actually be present as you taste, chew, swallow. This act, eating in silence or eating in sound, does define the experience. If you do not talk while you eat, read, drive, stand, pet the dog, or look out the window, it frees you to feel the textures, taste the flavors before swallowing. Each bite can be thus. The motion your jaw makes when eating or talking is a root act for humans that in a spare environment like a retreat becomes noticeable.

In fact, many traditions in the world make room for retreat, a place apart from normal distractions. The long and short of it is you catch, if you are lucky, glimpses of grace. Mostly, people find what pings around inside their heads a cacophony of unnecessary, competing thoughts. My husband uses meditation to settle and center him; it allows him to face the world mindfully in order to connect with other people in his life. I recognize the sentiment from the (mostly unspoken) Indian tradition in my childhood home and realize my American husband is tapping into a rich, deep practice advocated by Hindus, Buddhists, Christians, Muslims, Jews, American Indians, and almost any culture with a mystic, contemplative element in its history.

In India there is the idea of Om, a pulsing underlayer of universal sound, and it cannot be heard without quieting the senses—all six of them, if you include the mind as a sensory organ. We mimic this sound in our church music, in our chanting, in our speech, without realizing it. I remember and can feel the reverberating tones of song in a cathedral, the glowing light and towering spires pulling everything inside—tune and voice, heart and soul—upward. In Bali my husband and I once watched and listened to two hundred Hindu monks chanting to the night sky. Their circling, rhythmic voices enmeshed with the very air, swirled, pulsated, and strummed something under my breastbone. Historically in the United States, music was thought so powerful it could not be tolerated outside of church. Drumming, the music of black African slaves outlawed in the south in early US history, was considered far too dangerous. Connection to grace, and to one another, was powerful and best subdued.

As most of us know, a tune can evoke a memory, piercing faster and with more stealth than any conversation. I wish it weren't the case, but Cyndi Lauper's "Girls Just Want to Have Fun" takes me to Tunisia: 1985, a hotel rooftop restaurant overlooking a market in the capital, dry wind blowing in my face while I eat a steaming bowl of couscous. I heard the song on a European radio station, and after twelve months of Arab music it startled me. I had spent a year submerging my own beliefs to those of the culture where my husband and I were posted by the Peace Corps. I made no demands that the women there should think or behave as I did. When I heard that song, though, and looked around at all the women veiled and wrapped in *safsaris* walking along a road as they left the market bus, I suddenly wanted to scream the words aloud. To hold up a safsari, women clamp one end of a long white cloth in their teeth, making speech impossible.

I was at the hotel only because I was leaving the next day as a delegate to the 1985 United Nations Decade for Women Conference in Nairobi, Kenya, and all during the trip, I heard the song's reverberation. *Some people take a beautiful girl, hide her away from the rest of the world . . .* After arriving in Kenyatta Airport and taking a taxi to the conference area, I saw little groups of women from all over, little islands of culture, dress, and language, seriously addressing serious issues of development, the key idea being that if you empower females in a society, they in turn ensure proper nutrition, health, and education for their families. The North African group was the only one I saw with men standing about to protect their women from the rest of us. *Just wanna, just wanna.*

The vibration of speech, as well as music, has power. To this day, the particular vibration of Bengali makes me feel at ease, even if I hear it in passing in a grocery store. Once, during a business phone call to a man in Connecticut, I recognized the exact cadence of voice of my maternal uncle, Sujit, and immediately relaxed—that voice meant amused and interested conversation, a childhood in northern India, boarding schools, and family like mine. Instantly, I knew he was from Bengal, was probably educated in Kolkata, worked abroad, celebrated the same festivals we did, and ate the same comfort foods. I connected that cadence and sweep of sound to a long cultural story that nuanced my entire life.

People bandy words. Foods, spices, and phrases cross cultures, geography, and time. They develop new meanings or hold steadfastly to the old, create bridges or become familiar separations. In fact, all we know of the world comes from verbal and gastronomic stories. The geographical barriers of rivers, mountains, deserts, and forests once made it difficult for languages and cuisines to mingle and hence, even today, languages and menus across the world are very different from one another.

Recently, as an experiment, I measured how much time I spoke aloud and how much time I spent eating in a day. By my clock, out of the sixteen available hours in my day (I counted eight hours for sleep), I spoke for eight of them and ate for nearly half that time—three and a half hours. Ordinarily, I would not have given this a thought, but now, as one thought among many zipping through my head, it makes me a little tired and a little appalled at how much time I spent eating. Not only that, but I clearly see that I have twisted my tongue, translated meaning, responded to others in the imperfect system of language for half of my waking life. No wonder most major religions have a tradition of silent retreats. The spaces that make up the world, between trees and air, between stars and horizon, within our own body particles: wordless.

RAITA (BEATEN YOGURT WITH SPICES)

16 ounces plain yogurt
1 small cucumber, peeled and grated
salt to taste
1 teaspoon ground cumin seeds, roasted
¼ cup fresh cilantro, finely chopped
½ green chili, very finely chopped (optional)

Mix all ingredients in a bowl and serve.

Variations:
Instead of the cucumber, add ¼ teaspoon black pepper and ¼ cup chopped walnuts, or ½ of a potato cooked, peeled, and cut into ¼-inch cubes, or a handful of *boondias* (tiny fried balls made from chickpea flour) from an Indian store.

PARTY-POPPING FRIED CASHEWS

½ pound raw cashews (can be found in most grocery store health food
   sections)
salt to taste (about ¼ teaspoon)
black pepper to taste

Heat about 1 inch of oil in a small frying pan. When hot, put in all the nuts
and stir-fry until medium brown. Drain nuts on paper towel or in a sieve,
sprinkle salt and pepper on them, and slide them onto a serving plate. Fantastic served warm.

12

On the Road with Amiya and Rani

In 1974, the year I was twelve, my grandparents came to Kansas. Even before my grandparents' arrival, my friends realized I had a separate culture at home, but the presence of a sari-clad grandmother and a grandfather with an Indo-British accent made it undeniable, more so when they began appearing around town.

My grandfather visited the local First Christian Church as a speaker about India. He appeared there very dapper, with a walking cane, tie, lightweight wool trousers belted high on his waist, a matching four-button vest, and suit coat. In India his voice boomed to me whenever he used it as an instrument to speak singsong to his grandchildren, and at the church I heard it conjure a cultured Bengali. I remember him saying "We in India," with his head thrust back and his jaw pulled tight on the second syllable, In*dia*. Then with impeccable timing, one hand on his vest pocket and the other on top of his cane, he bent forward at the waist and peered intently at a small child while drawling, "you see." All it needed was a monocle for pure theater. Straightening, he continued, "We believe in a different sort of . . ." and I forget the rest in the memory of how he smiled while pulling his lips down at the corners, of how his eyes twinkled. The congregation received him well. They liked his charm, his Old World air. No one knew a thing about his life, nor did anyone ask, content with satisfying surface curiosity.

Amiya Kumar Banerji was an administrator for close to forty years. Sometimes he worked for industry, sometimes for the government of India. He took his family on his postings around India, living in one place for two years, or perhaps up to four years. My mother went to seven schools before she was eighteen. She learned English while attending Catholic English-medium schools to avoid having to learn a new language with each crossing of a state line, as each state in India was formed from an old kingdom with different languages and customs. The *mamas* (maternal uncles)—*baromama, mejomama,* and *chautomama* (oldest uncle, middle uncle, and youngest uncle)—all remember an idyllic four years in Dehradun in Uttar Pradesh from 1950 to 1954, when Amiya worked for the Forrest Research Institute. I saw one photo of the gardens and the house. Lush foliage and heavy fronds abound. It seems misty, a place apart, as if I am seeing it through a wash of rain on glass.

All through those years, Amiya and Pratibha (my grandfather called my grandmother "Rani," or queen, so consistently that many people did not know her actual first name) hosted parties and attended functions. They went or sent someone to market daily to pick out the best of the fish catch and the freshest in-season vegetables. Daily meals were always homemade and Didu supervised the cooking. During mango season, she many times made her special chutney using green mangoes. The taste was sweet and succulent, leaving a spicy tail-end snap on the tongue. The large glass jars of the chutney barely lasted until the next green mango harvest. My grandparents raised their four children eating it, they celebrated holy festivals with dabs of it on the sides of their plates, and they ate meals with it on the family table every day they could.

During these travel-and-work years, Dadu perfected his drawl when talking to small children. Didu chuckled with each performance. In the end, they settled in Ranchi, where my grandfather worked for the National Coal Development Corporation until his retirement. By the time he and my grandmother arrived for their visit to Kansas in 1974, Amiya was ready to see the world beyond India.

Because of this desire, we spent almost a month in our pea-green, pod-shaped Dodge Monaco pulling a camper trailer across the United States. Mom fed us packages of Cup-a-Soup that reconstituted with hot water. It was a brave new culinary world for my grandparents.

The trailer was one of those pop-up styles that had additional sleeping spaces in the portions that folded out. My grandmother, swathed in cotton saris to keep cool, had a time of it getting in and out. We stopped at KOA camping sites from Kansas to New York.

It was a private month in the Dodge for me. You wouldn't have thought so, not with my grandparents fresh from India with us, not with my brother, mother, and father in the car. The conversation in my memory is the same through Kansas as Missouri, the same through Missouri as Illinois—a roulette wheel of dialogue to spin, linger, and spin again. I tuned it out mostly. We went from Kansas to Chicago to New York to Washington, DC, and back, and it took us three weeks. Time spun out in wisps: the car hurtling through air, the bodies within it, the spinning conversations bubbling out of lips. The only solid thing was the stopping.

My mind focused sharply as the car took an exit ramp. This was Pennsylvania and acorns crunched under the car wheels as we drove under oaks and towering pines. After getting out, I casually kicked the gravel and got a bead on the coolers: with any luck Mom would deem the mayonnaise too far gone in the egg salad. The wooden picnic benches the park provided had a scattering of pine needles on them and there was a bird dropping on one of the planks. Chipmunks inquisitively snacked on acorns, sneaking looks at us as Mom pulled out a Tupperware container. I tensed.

Somehow the egg salad was still fine. She made sandwiches on white bread and handed around cups of water. Then it was back to hours of looking at the back of the driver's seat, telephone poles, cows, and billboards. For sport, my brother and I poked each other, trying to provoke an outburst. We proceeded across the country in this manner.

It was the KOA stores with their small figurines of the state we were in that brought me out of myself. With a sense of excitement I'd see the array of figurines, the key chains for Abby, for Beth, and though I don't remember ever seeing my name in a display, I always looked. Nancy was closest. I always looked for my brother, too. Sandy was sometimes there, never Sandeep, more proof that we were connected to another land. The best stores would have a pinball machine in a corner, and a freezer with prewrapped ice-cream treats. For some reason, I seemed to always have four dollars in my pocket and now I know it was because my grandfather gave it to me each time. I collected a small statue of two bears on a cross section of wood holding up an "I love Pennsylvania" sign, and a gold Empire State Building pencil sharpener. I usually left with my four dollars, but it was the possibility of spending it that was so wonderful.

The culinary differences between my two nations crystallized for me at a truck stop. As we made our way along the interstate, we stopped for an afternoon break in southern New York. I played with a thick white ceramic mug with no saucer, moving it along the blue Formica table until my mother gently touched my wrist. The table was attached to the wall at one end but the other was curved and wrapped with a strip of chrome. The bright sunlight reflected off the silver. Large windows, hot with the afternoon heat, made my mother turn her head away from the asphalt parking lot filled with Chevy Impalas, trucks, and our own Dodge. My grandparents took the seats farthest from the hot sunlight. They had spent a lifetime avoiding hot sun and were not about to bask in it in the United States. The waitress tapped her pencil.

"Is the water really hot for hot tea?" Mom asked with a hopeful expression.

"Sure." The waitress rubbed her knuckles along her notepad.

"Not just the coffee water, but boiling?" Mom tried a smile.

"It's really hot."

The tea bag came, as it had in Missouri, in Illinois, across Ohio and Pennsylvania, already undone in a piping-hot tin pitcher that somehow held only tepid water. There was never any milk or cream. The resulting drink had none of the personality of its namesake. Across the country, coffee was always a better bet. Mom's spoon clinked on the sides of her cup, paper napkins rustled in our shifting laps, the waitress looked as if she might need the table for the next diners, and men in plaid shirts across the way talked through and around the toothpicks in their mouths. My mother sighed a little as she took her first sip.

This teatime must have been strange for my grandparents. Teatime on my grandparents' veranda on a quiet street in India was a different thing altogether. I remember one afternoon, the unoon, unseen in the kitchen, heated water for tea—it had to bubble strongly for several minutes before it was deemed hot enough to brew tea properly—and milk and sugar sat at the ready. On the small table between rattan chairs outside was a plate of Nice brand biscuits, rectangle shaped with fluted edges. The sun was strong but filtered through latticework on the side of the house and I could see Tagore Hill in the distance, the garden wall twenty feet out, and exotic flora directly in front that curled green tendrils toward the light. Something broad-leaved and deep green glistened on my right. The wrought-iron gates to the property were down the drive. Inside, fans swirled the air from the ceiling and some of that breeze came through the latched screen doors. A lizard held still on the wall, then flashed away.

I was the only one awake other than Kamla. The others were taking an afternoon nap in deference to the sun and heat of midday. Not used to such a schedule, I read. As the smooth tiles cooled my feet, I glanced up once in a while at the tufted sides of Tagore Hill. The heat caused a haze that smudged the edges of the horizon beyond. Over a great deal of time, the hill had lost craggy rocks from its brow and those lay near the base now like giant jagged stepping stones. A rambling structure still stood about halfway up, molded over, its arches easily seen from my grandmother's house. Hikers stood on its flat roof and I wondered if it would hold their weight. I decided it would, at least another hundred years or so, as everything here seemed to last and last.

Kamla brought the tray of tea, her sandals slapping the floor. I liked the biscuits with the slight coconut taste so much it was hard not to clean the plate. I dipped the edge of a biscuit into the tea and later scooped the mush out from the bottom of the cup with the tiny spoon. While I sat in the warm sun, a vegetable seller stopped by with his basket to see if Didu would choose any items for dinner. Kamla's son, Mukund, proudly pointed out particular flowers in the garden he tended. There was no rush, no urgency.

The next afternoon as we sat around Didu's table at four o'clock, there was more than plain tea on offer. The hot, milky sweet tea was spiced with cardamom, ginger, black pepper, and cloves and the table sported spicy green beans, a platter of mustard fish, and plain rice in a scalloped bowl. Salty *neemki* nestled in a side bowl. My dadu ate the fish and green beans with rice and then began looking around the table. Didu ladled out the freshly made yogurt she started each night and left to form on the kitchen windowsill and offered the bowl to Dadu. He mixed the yogurt with rice and put a spoonful of chutney on his plate. The contrast in tastes had him smacking his lips. To me, this was four o'clock comfort. While it was a soft, questing time for adults to check in on what the plans for the evening were, how you were feeling, what you would like to eat, the table flavors made you sit up and notice.

As Lizzie Collingham notes in *Curry: A Tale of Cooks and Conquerors*, tea has been extremely popular in India since the British East India Company began its marketing push over a hundred years ago, but the story of tea began in China in the fourth century. From there, it spread to Japan, where it became an important social ritual, and also into Tibet and the Himalayan regions north of India, where it was consumed in a buttery soup. Hill tribes in Assam and farther east in Burma and Thailand chewed steamed and fermented tea leaves, but on the whole, Indians were not interested. Collingham writes, "When the interpreter for the Chinese Embassy of Cheng Ho visited Bengal in 1406, he was surprised to note that the Bengalis offered betel nuts to their guests rather than tea." But in my family, tea reigned high.

Though tea is popular in the United States now—at good coffee shops chai tea (which makes me smile, as the word *chai* means "tea") is often written in chalk on the menu board; there are loose-leaf black, green, white, and herbal teas; and when you order, tea comes with a pot of truly steaming water—in 1974, it was a disappointment during our trek across the country with my grandparents. Amiya and Rani had teatime at Rani Villa in mind. Nowadays, the growing interest in the United States in flavors, foodstuffs, and table traditions from elsewhere makes finding a good cup of tea a little less daunting. The afternoon rhythm of tea at Rani Villa? Ceiling fans wapping softly, unhurried sipping to gear up for what the evening would bring, the feeling of settling softly into the rest of the day. Tea held no such comforts in Kansas in the seventies, or at any of the interstate stops during my grandparents' visit to the United States. Other than inside the haven of Mom's own kitchen it was a tepid and slouchy version of itself. Good, hot black tea and its remarkable organizing effect on the day was one more casualty of immigration for my parents.

MOSHLA CHA (TEA WITH A MIXTURE OF SPICES)

Serves 6

Mixture to make ahead of time and use as needed for tea:
4 tablespoons ground ginger
2 tablespoons whole black peppercorns
2 tablespoons green cardamom seeds
1 tablespoon whole cloves
pot of tea
milk and sugar to taste

Grind the spices in a clean coffee grinder. Store the mixture in an airtight container and add ½ teaspoon to a pot of hot water, add tea leaves, and steep for 3 to 5 minutes. Strain as you pour into cups and serve with milk and sugar.

Or, to make moshla cha by the pot:
>4 cups water
>16 whole cardamom pods, slightly crushed
>2 cinnamon sticks
>½ cup milk
>3 ounces strong black tea leaves
>sugar to taste

Bring the water to a boil in a large pan and add the cardamom and cinnamon sticks. Simmer for 15–20 minutes. In a separate pan bring the milk to just below boiling and set aside. Add the tea leaves to the boiling water and then remove from the heat. Steep for 3–5 minutes. Strain the leaves and spices and add the milk and sugar to sweeten. Serve immediately.

DOI (HOMEMADE YOGURT)

Makes (2) 16-ounce containers

½ gallon whole or nonfat milk, as fresh as possible, at room temperature
2–3 tablespoons plain yogurt with active yogurt cultures, at room temperature
kitchen thermometer with clip

Carefully heat milk in a stockpot until it just begins to foam, then remove from heat. Next, cool the milk to 110°F, mix in the plain yogurt, and cover with a warm heating pad or towel. Or, heat your oven to 110–115°F, turn off the heat, place yogurt on the upper rack, and leave the pilot light on to maintain 90–110°F. Wait 7 hours, or overnight. The longer the yogurt sits, the thicker and more tangy it will become. Stir and pour into containers with tight lids, cover, and refrigerate. Yogurt will stay fresh for 2–3 weeks.

❖ ❖ ❖

NEEMKI (FRIED SALTY SNACK)

1 cup flour
4 tablespoons ghee or butter
¼–½ teaspoon salt
2 teaspoons water
½ teaspoon onion seeds
1 cup oil
flour for rolling

Mix the flour and salt and sieve into a medium bowl. Add ghee, onion seeds, and water to flour mixture and form a dough ball. Sprinkle a little flour onto a clean surface and knead the dough for 4–5 minutes. Roll the dough out into a large circle. Cut into ½-inch strips and then cut diagonally to form 1- to 2-inch pieces. Fry in hot oil until golden. Drain and serve. When cool, neemki can be stored in an airtight container for several days.

13

All Our Tupperware Is Stained with Turmeric

About three miles from our house, I sighted my horizons with an outstretched thumb and forefinger and squinted at undulating wheat. I had ridden my bike, passing edge-of-town neighborhoods, then clusters of scrubby trees, to reach a gravel road. I liked the idea I could be in Missouri soon if I kept going, and it was a good spot to be alone. I slid off the bike seat and walked to the edge of the field, sticking my palms out flat at my sides and twirling a bit with my head back. Tassels tickled my skin and my world shifted between sky and treetop and sky.

I swung for a while and frowned. On Saturday, at one of Mom's house parties, an auntie had used the royal "we" to exclude me. "We wear this saffron color at puja. We feel it is auspicious." It had seemed humorous at the time, that the Indian adults did not know what to do with my Americanized self, but now I wasn't so sure.

At sixteen, I wanted nationhood to include me. I wanted the vocabulary of belonging. I wanted it more than friendship, more than social ease. The weight of living in the Midwest, with its attendant school assemblies, church discussions, tetherball competitions, and more, left me looking Indian and feeling Indian in an ocean of otherness.

It didn't help that the week before I had recognized something new when with my friends. I rode in the backseat of a car as we trolled up and down the Broadway strip after school as usual. Work traffic was not yet out. Cars turned left onto side streets sporadically and we sipped limeades from Sonic. The greater adult world struggled with economic problems and tensions in Iran that, a mere twelve months later, set the stage for Ayatollah Khomeini's rule. But our fathers were all employed, we all had our first cars, and our big decisions included what to wear to homecoming and whether to stay in band. Other than the flashy new Pontiac Trans Ams that some Iranian students from Pittsburg State College drove, which caused teenage boys up and down the strip to frown in disgust, it seemed as if the outside world had little connection to us.

The air was warm, and crackling bunches of dry leaves rolled against the curbs. There we were: a ramshackle gathering of my friends, slouching and shifting so everyone could fit in the car. I was on the golf team in school, editor of the newspaper, and soon to be president of the student council. I knew everyone in our class of 250. I liked most of them. Then, our car passed Lloyd loping down the sidewalk near Fourth and Broadway. Lloyd was a shy black boy, endearing to me because papers and books seemed to be on the verge of falling out of his grasp all the time, and because his curly black hair bounced a little as he walked. In the car, my friend since kindergarten cracked a joke about blacks and the carful of teens laughed. It wasn't the first time this had happened. This time, though, the joke had a specific target. I balled my fists. My brown skin stretched. Laughter filled the car, an elbow clipping me in the ribs to indicate our sisterhood in this, and I receded into myself, narrowed my eyes, and looked straight ahead.

As usual when annoyed, I began cataloging details of appearance. My friend who had made the joke crossed her arms over her belly. She thought she was getting fat and that this posture helped hide it. There was acne on her face, one really large, unseemly zit near her nose. And today, she wore a new top that made her uncomfortable and so she kept scratching at her sleeves. My mind spun out more observations, trying on and flicking off reasons that would cause her to joke in such a way.

A day or two later, my friends came around when they missed our group and our episodes of aimless teenage plans. I wasn't done mulling over their behavior. I continued to read thick novels like *Clan of the Cave Bear* and finished a book a day until I was ready to deal with them. I developed a fierce concentration that was broken only when my mother talked directly to me.

"Phone call," she'd say, startling me out of my fictitious world. I would just shake my head. I did not have the language needed to talk to them.

I did go out again to the country-western dance bar, and again to the old coal strip-mine pits for parties. But when I saw those friends again at Sonic and shared rides to school in the morning, I noticed something in the way they plucked at their fingers until the skin was red and flaky near the nails, held their schoolbooks against their ribs, pulled their lips over straightened teeth like a thin skin stretched tight over a drum. The underlying vibration that I felt so keenly, the one that absolutely did not allow for belittling, was lost to them in all but suspicion. I would never again look at others outside a group, outside a culture or a political viewpoint, in the same way. A great stubbornness arose in me to hold my ground. I am That; a whisper of old wisdom coiled through my thoughts. And stuck.

As I swung my arms at the edge of the wheat field, I had an idea for bridging my two homelands. Mom and I would make an Indian feast for my ninth-grade friends and they would begin to understand all the wonder of my world. That weekend we cooked our regulars: dal, cumin green beans, tomato chutney, chicken curry, and because it was a special night, chops. I set the table with Mom's cream lace tablecloth, china, and napkins. I aligned the heavy dining chairs along the table, dusted the china cabinet, and twitched the green silk curtains back and forth to find the best placement over the pale green wallpaper patterned with white flocking. Then we began to fry luchis, and warm bread aroma filled the air.

Six girls came at 6:00 P.M. There was a flutter of conversation and eventually we all settled in the dining room. I brought in steaming platters and told my friends about the Indian custom of eating the vegetables and dal first, then the meat curry. I told them about tomato chutney and how the black mustard seeds popped in the hot oil before Mom and I put in the tomatoes. How I added sugar and raisins and let the chutney cool before adding lemon to make it tart-sweet for them. Tomato chutney is like a cleanser for the palate between foods, I told them. There was a pause. Serving bowls were passed around and utensils picked up.

"Now," P— said, "what *is* this exactly," and she poked her fork into succulent chicken. It was as if she suspected something unpalatable. I looked down the table to my mother and hated that she heard my friend's tone. P— pushed her food to one side.

The rest of the table was quiet and I forced a laugh.

After the meal, I was done introducing my friends to Indian food. Everyone was more comfortable in the land of burgers and fries. Paper holders for salty fries at the DQ, white-flour buns, a thin disk of beef, yellow cheese, ketchup, mustard, and two fluted slices of dill pickle. That was the sum of comfort. My comfort, taste, and aroma of home were held exotic, foreign to my friends. I had been right to keep them safe behind our front door. Never again would I tolerate skeptical poking at Mom's fabulous chicken. The next day, Sunday, I asked for mangsho (meat) curry made from minced meat and tiny cubes of potatoes served with rice, and sandesh for dessert. Even though Mom had just made a large feast, my favorites appeared anyway and soothed. Stepping out of our pocket of culture had not gone so well and I would not try again until venturing out of the United States.

KEEMA (COMFORTING MINCED MEAT CURRY)

Serves 4

2 tablespoons vegetable oil

1 bay leaf

4 whole cloves

4 whole cardamom pods

½ stick cinnamon

1 dried red chili

1 medium onion, finely chopped

½ teaspoon sugar

1 pound lean minced meat (lamb or beef)

1 inch of fresh ginger root, finely chopped or mashed, or 1 teaspoon dried ginger

¼–½ teaspoon cayenne or to taste

1 teaspoon salt

1 medium potato, peeled and cut into small ½-inch cubes, or ¾ cup frozen peas

¼–½ teaspoon garam masala (optional)

Heat the oil in a medium-sized, heavy pan. When hot, add bay, cloves, cardamom, cinnamon, and dried chili and let sizzle for 5 seconds. Add chopped onions and fry until the edges start to turn brown. Push onions to the side and add sugar to the oil. Let the sugar heat through and begin to caramelize, stirring a little, before mixing it into the rest of the onions. Add the minced meat and fry until browned. If needed, drain excess fat. If using potatoes, add them now. Add ginger, cayenne, and salt. Continue to fry, stirring frequently to avoid sticking, about 10 minutes. Add enough water to come just to the top of the meat. If using peas, add them now. Reduce heat and simmer uncovered 15 minutes. Keema should be moist, with a little "sauce," not completely dry. If desired, add garam masala. Serve with rice or Indian bread, luchi [see recipe on page 56] or roti [see recipe on page 55].

The recipe for the soothing sandesh mentioned in this chapter is on page 14.

14

Strength of a Nation

Kansas life was encompassing and my connection to India waned. I liked our food but I had no other calling card. I had aged out of that grace period of youth when all I had to do was eat a sweet and grin at my parents' Indian friends. Relatives, especially, expected more of me now. I began to note that this thing called nation was pervasive: it made songs I knew nothing of, prized collective memories of past sagas, created scenes a whole community of people remembered. Those communal memories were fractured nightly in India with television pictures of temples bombed, mosques burned, and trains attacked by religious extremists. There was a high cost to losing these shared ties. When they were gone, citizen turned against citizen.

It had been seven years since I had been in India. We were going again, and leading up to our 1977 journey, nearly one thousand political opponents of Indira Gandhi had been jailed, and a program of compulsory birth control had been introduced. Gandhi's Congress Party lost and then won again in the general elections. Pakistan, on the northwest border, had declared martial law. Tensions were high and in late 1978, Gandhi herself was arrested and jailed for contempt of parliament. All these events set the stage for political splinter groups and continuing shows of might so that by 1984 even the Golden Temple, the Sikhs' most holy shrine, was stormed to flush out Sikh militants pressing for self-rule. Then Gandhi was assassinated by her Sikh bodyguards. Bollywood movies, universally watched and commented upon in India, could tie the population to favorite songs and stories for intervals in darkened theaters, but the times called for more than cinema unity.

In the late 1970s India meant different things to each neighbor in my grandparents' town in Bihar. If the strength of a nation is simply the idea it evokes, I saw I wasn't really part of India: just someone ringing the doorbell. My ideas of India were once removed, secondhand. I had no lifetime of ordinary daily experiences there. *Deshies* (Indians living abroad) were hard pressed to find a place in the subcontinent. I included India in my heart and mind but I found it did not include me.

This was unbearably embarrassing, and so at sixteen, I did not want to return to India. Teenage instinct told me how out of place I would be. My pride in the idea of being Indian now failed me. I had seen this happening at the Indian events we attended in Kansas City. There were no other teens at the parties because the families had had their children later than my parents, the smaller children were occupied in their own ways, and I couldn't quite hang out with the adults. I knew that in India my parents would take us visiting as usual, and rituals that used to work for me as a child there, primarily eating sandesh, somehow would not work now. At sixteen, I was neither child nor adult, and there was shaky protocol for all else. But I hid these fears and packed a suitcase for our family vacation. I knew I would hate the trip.

The food at Didu's house, however, was amazing. In fact, our first meal included delicate and flaky yogurt fish, *doi maach*, and the bitter gourd, korola, that I remembered calling blood purifier with my father with a giggle because it seemed to scour all other flavors from my mouth. Didu associated healthy properties with bitter korola gourd and it is, in fact, a Bengali favorite made with other vegetables in a dish called *shukto*. And though my youthful palate shuddered, Didu skillfully balanced the bitterness with the flavors of the other vegetables and mustard seeds. Still, I kept my eyes down when I took a tiny taste to give my tongue time to settle down. Somehow the rice, the other vegetables, or maybe just the situation of being at my didu's table softened the bitter bite. After the shukto, the flavor of the flaky fish was outstanding, and perhaps the contrast was the point all along.

It seemed all we did was eat. In the early evening, my grandparents would walk with us to visit a neighbor or two and we would be offered sweets and tea and more sweets. The talk would wind and drift and my grandfather would begin to explain why I was so tan. "She stays too much in the sun," he would say, often shaking his head. I realized with a start that even here, skin tone was a point of reflection.

Even though we visited a lot of people, it seemed an individual act of courage to greet an older family friend every time. Once, when I bent to touch the toes of an uncle in pronam, the traditional greeting to a respected elder, he scowled and I felt a change in the air around me. I glanced quickly at the photo of this man on the side table. No, his face wasn't usually scrunched in such a fashion. I had heard Uncle was fifty-five years old and newly retired. My father had snorted at such a notion, *what will he do with himself?* I felt sad looking at the tidy apartment. He had a daily schedule consisting of a walk to the market, to the tobacco shop, and perhaps after greeting his neighbors, a cup of tea to accompany the newspaper. Maybe his scowl reflected his distaste of my Americanness, or maybe it was because he sensed my lack of knowledge of India, that I hadn't pressed to know our language enough, or perhaps he was merely anticipating his afternoon nap. I could not say. After the traditional pronam, there was usually a round of smiles and shaking heads and words to the effect of "no, no, child, no need for that." With this uncle, something wasn't sitting right. I had already committed to the downward plunge to touch just the tip of his toes with my finger: I aimed for the right big toe, then the left, after which I brushed my forehead and heart with my fingers. I wasn't ever sure if these were exactly the right spots, but no one really looked that closely, so it worked. Yet he did not seem happy I had done pronam. I know he saw that I lacked the sureness of belonging.

It was difficult at all the temples we visited, too. Ritual is important in temples; in fact their architecture and floor plans are built from it; they are festooned in it constantly and lovingly. It is their reason for being there at all. Garlands of flowers hang in certain places, put there in morning rituals. You pray in a certain fashion at certain times and listen with certain postures. It is silent, except when it is not and then you might hear conch shells blowing. The catch was I needed to understand the meaning of these rituals for them to make any sense. Because I was blindly following a parent, it all seemed awkward. The priest would pour holy water only into my right palm, a fact I learned while standing in front of a frowning priest. It was important to eat all the *prasad* (food eaten symbolically for God), which

I learned as I was trying *not* to have to eat all of mine, and just gazing at a *murti*, a god-image, should have provoked a host of holy stories in my mind to help fortify my spirituality in this world. Unlike the Christians I knew in Kansas, Hindus loved more than one story and enjoyed complex plots. Since my parents had not actually told me any of the Hindu stories, the murtis were just figures to me; they did not help me focus my mind. The stories behind them were vague, and so one set of figures meant about the same thing to me as another. Once, I saw the niches lined up on either side of the approach to a northern Indian temple. The walk was white stone, as were the temple, the niches, and arches. It all had the aspect of a floating cloud of smooth, milky marble. The walk was tidily lined with various figures: Ganesh, Hanuman, Jesus, Krishna, Durga, Lakshmi, Saraswati. I felt an odd jolt seeing Jesus there, his face tipped peacefully to the side, his hand held up as I had seen in Christian churches at home. He was among world avatars here, messengers, enlightened beings trying to share a message of faith. I passed many such figures on the way inside, each story aimed to help until knowledge and compassion, represented by the inner sanctum, could enliven the world.

We went to see a southern Indian temple in the middle of the hurly-burly city of Tiruchchirappalli. Unlike the northern temple, this temple's outside walls were covered in all manner of human and animal figures doing the things man and beast do in this world—playing, working, fighting. Each carved limb was painted a vibrant color. Each carved figure smoothly held the toes or torso of another above it. These stone carvings, several millennia old, depicted myriad worldly distractions that trick people into forgetting true human nature, the same distractions that constantly trick us into believing in the duality of beings. Visitors passed under the arches swollen with carvings of these ideas until they reached a quiet, still center where they might, if ready, catch grace.

On one temple visit, we marched up 108 steps (representing the 108 names of God) toward a temple built on a steep rise and found an elephant under an arched hall. How he got up those people-sized steps, I do not know. My father gave his handler some coins and gently pushed my brother and me forward. I stepped toward him, my eyes on his large feet. He fidgeted and I froze. His nails were yellowish and thick and capped some heavyweight toes. In the end, the photo shows me in a slight bow partly because I was trying to keep my feet as far away as possible from the behemoth. The elephant is tapping the top of my head with his trunk in a blessing.

Indians revere elephants for their memory. Handlers work tirelessly to make sure they are treated well, have what they need, and are not overworked. Many temples support an elephant and in the south of India there is an annual Elephant Parade between temples. There are few wild elephant herds left in India, but in recent years some of those herds have rampaged through villages with uncharacteristic violence. Some villagers and others attribute it to the elephants' irritation at increasing human encroachment into wild lands. The elephants' memory is such that they know something has been taken away.

When I finally returned to the States a month later, I was certain I was happy to be home again. I craved the four-square orderliness of Pittsburg, the leafy catalpa trees, the curbs lining the streets. Yet when we returned, I was at sea. India had pulled my breastbone apart and left my beating heart exposed. Neighborhood friends frowned when I started to speak about the trip. My fascination seemed wrong to them. I spun between nations, and so I retreated. Once again, I hid my Indianness behind a wall.

Not long ago, thirty years after the elephant blessed me, I had another chance to visit Indian temples. My father, who was eighty-one at the time, told me he wanted to visit some of the holy places in India. A longing emerged in me so severe that I immediately agreed to go. At last, a tangible place for refuge, for explanations of a greater being, for what all the ritual of India was teaching. I thought back to grade school and all the questions I had had. Trips to India had always held out the promise of answers. This time, my mother was to go as well and I readily accepted the role of helper. The oldest temple on our route, Tirupati, a southern Indian temple so ancient that some estimates put it at 5000 BCE, caught my imagination from the first.

Tirupati sits atop a mountain. At its base is a bustling city with *gopurums* (temple gates) visible from most corners. A road winds upward through the Tirumala Hills to the temple. The trip lifted us all out of ourselves, partly because our driver screeching around corners caused ideas to surface about life and death, and partly because there was something of anticipation and joy in the air. In earlier centuries, the walk up this same hill would have created days to build anticipation. In an hour, about halfway up the modern blacktop road, our driver seemed to settle into a calmer rhythm, but I kept my hand clutched around the door handle nonetheless. My mother and father reminded me that inside the temple I should observe silence. They cautioned me not to speak, or my accent would give me away. Only Hindus were allowed on the grounds, which my parents didn't think was a good tradition, but there it was, and since not many Hindus without an Indian regional accent visited here I needed to keep my Kansas tongue still. This was, in fact, overly cautious on their part, but my parents were adamant that the local temple staff would look at foreign accents with suspicion. Stillness was better for me in any case. Without speech, I could better sense the beat of history that seemed tangible here.

Seven thousand years ago these traditions were already so entrenched that Vedic teachers built this temple, on top of a hill, out of stone, to commemorate them and to encourage seekers on their journeys. How many elephants had it taken to drag the rock, and how many stonecutters to create the blocks? In silence, I could breathe in that majestic, sublime sweep of history, of the modern-day visitors, hundreds of thousands of them, who worshipped here every year and brought their faith and love to its altars.

The temple grounds began unprepossessingly with modern housing units, parking lots topped with tarmac, and pilgrims in various groups heading toward the temple's cobblestoned outer approach. At the car, we removed our shoes and quick-stepped across the hot parking lot. Once we neared the outer buildings, the ancient world opened up. A great expanse of old cobblestone, cooler on the toes than the sun-heated tarmac, stretched before us as large as two football fields. On the far side, the temple proper was fronted by carved facades. Tirupati, like many temples built by the ancients, had an inner courtyard and meditation niches with arched openings for teaching and sitting. Inside the walls, too, was an inner sanctum encased in a separate building with a carved cupola on top. It housed the god-image Venkateswara, a form or incarnation of Vishnu in this age, and paid homage to grace. From where we stood, however, we could see only a tall, dark stone fortress.

Alongside the temple facade was a great, shallow, rectangular-shaped lake with broad stone steps on all four sides graduating down to the water. Temple priests performed ceremonies there using fire and water, my mother said. The grounds were full of people, too. Milling crowds filled the cobblestone area, a hundred people were gathered and seated around a priest chanting on a dais, and fifty in wide red skirts twirled like dervishes around a ring of drummers. Barefoot people walked about in white cotton, like my father, or in saffron and other vibrant colors, like my mother and me. I soaked it up as we walked slowly forward. Something about the quality of the light and air made distance hard to judge. It took nearly fifteen minutes to get close to the temple walls. I noticed the priest now held a colorful banner, and smoking incense wafted from a *rath*, a raised platform. A procession commenced around the temple walls, reminding me of Catholic ceremonies half a world away. The crowd, blowing conch shells and tinkling bells, followed the Hindu priest around the temple walls in his daily ceremony of gratitude. We joined a line that wound around and through outer hallways to reach the inner sanctum.

Inside, it was silent but for the sounds of fabric rustling and bare feet slapping against stone. Before we came to the final arched door, a stream of water rushed over the floor to wash our feet. We wound slowly closer, past gold columns, gold walls, and a huge gold weigh scale should people be tempted to offer their weight or their baby's weight in gold for a blessing. The gold gleamed in the unlit room and reflected what light came through the arched stone doorway. I trailed my hand along a half wall as we moved forward. When we reached the inner sanctum I saw the temple deity, Venkateswara, dressed and bedecked in flowers, and the crowd silently surged. In Hinduism and other Eastern belief systems, the gods are avatars—not the source of energy but rather agents of it. They are how people conceive of the force that supports the world. The bedecked deity was but a manmade worldly image, a portal to the Kingdom, as Christians call it, and passing through marked the end of attachment to the material world.

I wondered what I was to feel here in this ancient spot. At first nothing much came to mind. I was crowded by people jostling, leaning forward, their heads tipped back to see the deity. I breathed deeply of the incense wafting upward. Nothing. Then I looked about and saw intense longing on the faces surrounding me, a grasping for, yet a simultaneous reaching outside of, individual experience. A curious desire enveloped me to join in this journey myself.

After centuries, the temple once again did its work, this time on me. It was like a beckoning hand: Begin the journey. Stay the course. Breathe.

DOI MAACH (YOGURT FISH)

Serves 4

1½ tablespoons vegetable oil
1 pound fresh, meaty fish such as halibut steaks
1 large bay leaf
3 small cardamom pods
3 whole cloves
1-inch cinnamon stick
1 onion, finely sliced
½ of a tomato, chopped
¾ cup yogurt, stirred; more if needed
1 teaspoon turmeric
½ teaspoon cayenne (or to taste)
¾ teaspoon ground ginger
1 tablespoon raisins
salt to taste
½ teaspoon sugar

Heat oil, slightly braise each side of fish pieces, and set fish aside (if fish is very fresh, this step is not needed). After removing fish from the pan, add ½ tablespoon oil to the pan. When hot, add bay leaf, cardamom, cloves, and cinnamon stick. Let the whole spices sizzle for 5 seconds. Add sliced onions and sauté until slightly golden brown. Into the yogurt add turmeric, ground ginger, and cayenne and stir until blended. Place fish in pan carefully, without breaking, and add yogurt mixture. Add raisins, sugar, and salt to taste. Cover and cook for 10 minutes on low heat until fish is cooked and yogurt gravy is thick. Serve with rice.

SHUKTO (BITTER GOURD WITH MIXED VEGETABLES)

Serves 4

1½ teaspoons mustard seeds, finely ground and mixed with 1 cup water

½ teaspoon turmeric powder

½ teaspoon cayenne, plus another ¼ teaspoon (optional)

handful of bari, about ⅛ cup (pureed, dried lentils made into small balls, available at Asian groceries; optional)

2 tablespoons vegetable oil

½ teaspoon panch phoron, plus another ¼ teaspoon (panch phoron, or five spice, can be found in Indian/Asian groceries)

1 dried chili pepper

½ bitter gourd, chopped into very small pieces

1 carrot, julienned and parboiled

1 medium-sized potato, boiled in its jacket and cooled overnight in the refrigerator

¾ cup green beans, cut to the length of the julienned carrots

salt to taste

½ cup water

½ teaspoon clarified butter

Peel the potato, cut it into small cubes, and set aside. Stir ground mustard seeds into 1 cup of water. Add turmeric and cayenne, mix well, and set aside. In a heavy saucepan, heat 1½ tablespoons oil. If using bari, add it now to the hot oil, and when it is slightly browned, remove from oil and set aside.

Add panch phoron to hot oil, then quickly add dried chili pepper, broken in half. Let the spices sizzle for 5 seconds, then add all the vegetables. Stir-fry for 3 minutes. Pour mustard, turmeric, and cayenne mixture into the pan with the vegetables. Add ½ cup water. Add salt to taste and heat through. In a small pan, heat clarified butter, add ¼ teaspoon panch phoron, and let sizzle for 10 seconds. Add ¼ teaspoon cayenne if desired, immediately take pan off the heat, and add the mixture to the vegetables. Add bari just before serving. Serve shukto with rice.

15

Street Foods

Some stories evoke untroubled times, golden days that transport your mind, make you forget everything but the tenderness and exhilaration of those far-flung images. While attending the Bihar College of Engineering in Patna from 1948 to 1952, my father went once in a while for coffee with friends. The India Coffee House charged one-quarter of a rupee for coffee. It was a princely sum to the young college students, but my father got all he could from the treat, adding milk and sugar to the coffee since it did not cost extra, cooling himself for as long as possible under the coveted ceiling fans over the tables. There, he discussed all manner of critical issues with friends. Their heads tipped together in discussion until a strong point caused a sensation, whereupon the men would rear back, raise their voices, and fling their hands up emphatically. Usually, though, the Coffee House was too expensive. For half the price, one-eighth of a rupee, Baba could get corn grilled in a charcoal oven by a street vendor, who first dribbled it in oil and then flavored it with masala. How delicious, how heady to stand and munch alongside the road. How rich the feeling of having enough coin for the act.

On family trips to India in the 1960s and '70s, though, all the adults would mutter dire things about cleanliness when confronted by street vendors and steered us away. I was told that only people who grew up eating those foods could get away with it now. The rest of us had stomachs too delicate for the job. So naturally, nothing spelled nation to me quite like munching street foods right from the cart. I was tortured by longing for the sizzling *aloo tikkas, puchkas,* and *shingaras* as we passed by.

Eating on your feet near a cart and a fryer can conjure place like no other act. The ingredients are local, as are most of the other eaters standing with their hands cupped around puchkas and aloo tikkas, my mother's favorites. The people stand in relaxed postures, shoulders hunched slightly until they toss their heads back to catch all the savory juices. The dishes are mostly quite fresh, and they are cheap. It is the same the world over. Picture bagel carts in New York, cheesesteak vendors in Philadelphia. In my hometown of Pittsburg, Kansas, I think of snow cones at Lincoln Park. A Tunisian baguette filled with a fried egg, potatoes, and *harissa* instantly makes me think of hot desert sun. Forget seating arrangements. You could only eat those sandwiches on the go. *Dhabas* serving *chaat,* India's savory, tart, hot, sweet street food, is at the heart of the country's food culture.

In the southern states, the *chaat* experience is not the same as in North India. In the south, street corner vendors dole out hot *idlis, medu vadas,* and oothappams or spread *dosa* batter thinly onto hot griddles. Shingaras (or samosas in Hindi), though, are available in most Indian states.

But in the north, chaat is a category by itself. Any variety of it is an enticing blend of four tastes—sweet, sour, pungent, and spicy. The word *chaat* is derived from the Hindi verb *chaatna,* meaning "to lick one's fingers clean" after eating a tasty dish. One story has it that chaat came from a concoction prepared and eaten by Punjabi merchants as they sat managing accounts for their retail and moneylending businesses. To pass the long work hours, the men would nibble at puffed rice and soon began to add things like jaggery, ginger, and tamarind chutney. The resulting food was tasty enough that they began to lick their fingers after eating.

One beloved chaat is puchka. A filling made of small potato cubes or mashed potatoes, masalas (spices or spicy sauces), and boiled chickpeas is placed within a broken puchka. The tiny round puchka, made of wheat flour and semolina, is deep-fried in oil until it puffs up into a firmly crisp, hollow ball. This ball is then punctured from the top, filled with potatoes, boiled chickpeas, or boiled bean sprouts, and dipped in water spiked with coriander, black salt, green chili paste, mint, cumin, and sometimes tamarind. In Delhi they call it *golgapa*, and in Mumbai it's *panipoori*. The water and fillings can be made more or less pungent according to taste.

Chaat wallahs (snack vendors) offer strained yogurt to ease digestion and serve green coriander chutney and sweet tamarind-date-jaggery chutney to perk up the flavors of chaat and entice your taste buds. And these never fail to do so.

I ate street food only when I wasn't with my parents. The memory of it now transports my mind, like my father's, to exhilarating times. My husband, Terry, and I went to India in 1986 after our two-year Peace Corps assignment, and for the first time in my life I saw India without a family filter. We rode buses, bought tourist-class train tickets, and sat for hours during the long overland journeys. En route, we discussed the United States with Indian schoolteachers on holiday, university researchers, and engineers on business trips. They clustered around my husband and asked thoughtful questions, gave inquisitive nods of encouragement as he talked, and generally made him feel welcome. I held back, viewing these encounters with the mass of travelers in India with trepidation. My family had kept my brother and me separated from other travelers. No buses, ever. No waits at train stations. No standing in line at ticket counters and chatting with those nearby. The ordinary ebb and flow of travel in India in those days was time consuming, sometimes dirty, and always chaotic. To lessen these stresses, we arrived by family car, had our bags deposited, and walked directly into our compartments. This time, I was in the India on the other side of the glass. The one that roiled with life and strife, the one that beckoned from beyond the window.

At the southwestern town of Cochin, Terry and I purchased samosas from a street cart. It was a rare treat, my first street vendor food (other than coconut milk in the north), and we reveled in the experience: the hovering patrons, the beeping motorized rickshaws, the sizzling morsels, and the gritty texture of pavement beneath our feet. The act of eating absorbed all the attention of the patrons. There was little talk. Since we had lived in North Africa for two years, our stomachs had linings like cast iron. We were now qualified to stop at any street stand with no fear and, oh, that taste was sweet. Next, we bought overnight accommodations at a government-run hostel. We crossed the bay by small boat and arrived at what was once an opulent palace. It had been built on an island, covering it entirely. While it had a bit of a neglected air, the marble "bones" were solid, sweeping, and elegant. I was transported to the era of the Raj; we drank tea and ate breakfast breads in the morning under the soft wap-wap of ceiling fans on the veined-marble, open-air veranda. Of all the images of that trip, I carry with me the hustling beep-beep of cars, the rickshaws, the maids with short straw brooms sweeping marble floors, samosas off a cart, and tea on a veranda. As it did for my father before me, food links me directly to place, and to the memory of untroubled days.

PUCHKA (CHICKPEAS IN TINY PUFFED BREADS WITH SPICES)

Serves 6–8

The night before you want to serve, grind the following and make a paste:
5–6 mint leaves, minced
2 tablespoons fresh cilantro, minced
1–2 green chilies, chopped
½ teaspoon cumin seeds
two shakes black pepper
½ teaspoon black salt (regular white salt can be used)

Put the paste into 2 quarts of water.

Add 2 tablespoons panipoori moshla (found in Indian food stores) and refrigerate overnight. Strain the water before serving.

Also, the night before:
Cook 1 large potato in its jacket. Cool and store in the refrigerator overnight.

For the puchka, knead the following until smooth, cover, and set aside 30 minutes:
1½ cups semolina (sooji)
1 teaspoon oil
1 teaspoon flour
salt
club soda
vegetable oil in a small, deep pan or wok to deep-fry the breads

Make grape-sized balls with the dough, press with a tortilla press, or roll with a rolling pin to about 1½ inches in diameter. Fry the resulting flat rounds in medium-hot oil until crispy. In the end they should be about the size of a ping-pong ball.

Or, buy ready-made puchkas at Indian grocery stores.

To serve:
Place one 16-ounce can of chickpeas (garbanzo beans) in a small serving bowl. Peel the potato, cube it into ½- to ¼-inch squares, and place in a small bowl. Keep the spiced water with a ladle and the small puchkas nearby. Place a puchka in your palm, puncture it with a thumb, put in one or two potato pieces and several garbanzos, and then dribble in the panipoori water. Add tamarind chutney or green coriander chutney if desired. Pop into your mouth. Napkins are needed!

ALOO TIKKA (SPICY POTATO PATTIES)

Serves 4

2 potatoes, peeled, boiled and mashed with a fork
¼ cup onion, finely chopped
1 green chili, finely sliced
1½ teaspoons salt
1 tablespoon vegetable oil

Mix all the ingredients in a small bowl and form 2- to 3-inch patties. Heat the oil in a heavy frying pan. When hot, place the potato patties in a single layer around the pan. When lightly browned, turn. Serve with taetul (tamarind/date chutney and/or coriander chutney) and slivers of raw onion.

TAETUL CHATNI (TAMARIND/DATE CHUTNEY)

16-ounce bag of ground, mashed dates (or whole dates, soaked in water
   for 2 hours and then blended in a food processor)
3 tablespoons tamarind paste
½ teaspoon salt
½–1 teaspoon cayenne pepper
½ teaspoon ground coriander
½ teaspoon ground cumin
2–3 tablespoons brown sugar, or gurr (palm sugar); adjust quantity
   as needed

Mix the above ingredients in a small bowl. Adjust spices to taste. Can be stored
in an airtight container in the refrigerator for 6 weeks.

The recipe for the cilantro chutney mentioned in this chapter is on page 29.

SHAG-PIANG PAKORA (SPINACH AND ONION FRITTERS)

Serves 4–6

1 cup chickpea flour
¼–½ teaspoon cayenne pepper
½ teaspoon salt, or to taste
½ cup water
3 tablespoons vegetable oil
8 ounces fresh spinach, chopped (frozen, defrosted spinach also works)
½ of an onion, thinly sliced

Mix the chickpea flour, cayenne powder, salt, and water in a small mixing bowl. Adjust spices to taste. In a separate bowl, mix the spinach and onions. Heat oil in a frying pan, and when hot gather a 1½- to 2-inch clump of the spinach and onions between your fingers and dip into the flour mixture to coat. Place batter-covered pakora into the hot oil and repeat until the bottom of the pan is filled. Fry pakoras until golden brown, turning to get all sides.

Serve warm with taetul chutney [see recipe on page 119] or fresh cilantro chutney [see recipe on page 29].

Variations: Use other vegetables of your choice, such as ¼-inch-thick sliced potatoes, cauliflower florets, onions by themselves, or whatever takes your fancy.

16

Six Recipe Cards, a Wing and a Prayer, Circa 1984

As with my grandmother and mother before me, an astonishing network of mothers, aunts, and cousins, epic really in its proportions, reached out to me in Kansas when I was seventeen in 1979. It was because of Indian boys. Other than my brother and a son of a family friend who had lived in Pittsburg and then moved, no Indian males my age had lived nearby for most of my life. Heads were no doubt scratched, brows furrowed. Then, as if by magic, one day an Indian boy arrived at the bus stop on Fourth Street.

He—a friend of a cousin of an aunt, I am sure—stumbled out of a bus to meet me, though this was never said directly, after a fourteen-hour-plus ride north from a university in Texas. He had been raised in India but had been in the United States a year or two, dressed well, and was a boy from a good family. Unfortunately, just before leaving, the young man had broken his arm in such a way that the position of the cast made him look as if he were taking the oath of office or reciting the Boy Scout pledge. Either way, I couldn't take him seriously. Seeing him turned sideways in order to get his upraised plastered arm out of the bus was enough.

After that, no other young Indian male visitors arrived and I was relieved that this form of linking my two worlds was abandoned. I was off to college, anyway. Who could have predicted that there, swiftly, I would meet and soon marry Terry, a Missouri man from a farming family? Talk about cultural leaps.

But not only did we marry, we left for the Peace Corps just after my gradua-tion. We both wanted to physically help in the world. Wisps of memory, too, caught at my attention and I realized, finally, that the young boy eating a banana through its bitter peel was not a dream. It took seventeen years for me to ask the question of my mom: Were we ever on a bus ride in the blue Nilgiri Hills together? I recognized the landscape she mentioned, the bus pullout where we stopped for juices—I recognized *him*. This had the astonishing effect of reshaping my mind. That sensation just under my sternum that animated all my opinions on politics and charitable efforts had a basis. I saw, too, that I could do something. I imagined that boy, if he had been well fed and secure, rolling his eyes. *Took you long enough.* So, though Terry and I had our own two cultures to juggle, we decided to add yet one more: Tunisia.

In June 1984, we left for a two-year assignment in the North African desert. I packed only essentials for Tunisia: two dresses, three long-sleeved cotton shirts, a pair of loose pants. Reluctantly, I left my cheesecloth for chhana folded at Mom's house and adjusted my expectations for desserts: no sandesh for two years. I tucked in a tiny sample of Clinique makeup next to the lining of my pack. I brought Rockport shoes, ugly and thick; a sun hat; a small flip notebook with "RECIDEX Recipe Organizer" printed to look like cross-stitch on its front.

I had written NINA MUKERJEE in all block letters on the inside cover of the four-by-three-inch notebook some years before and now I pulled it out while sitting facing my mother at the kitchen table in May 1984. Mom was folding laundry and I was sitting forward, concentrating, trying to get it all down before leaving the next month.

I could have relied entirely on the native foods of Tunisia, or on noo-dles or peanut butter from the commissary at the US embassy in Tunis, where I heard volunteers had access, but I copied out six recipes as I sat at our Kansas table: a curry for meats, green beans with cumin, tomato chutney, dal, *payesh*, and oatmeal cookies. The Indian recipes, I realize now, were the same ones for which my mother had written frantic letters to Didu when she left India for Thailand in 1960. They had emerged from her girlhood in India and mine in Kansas: softball and Slurpees, ballet and tap, clarinet and piano, so far removed from her doings but a tether to home just the same. For me, India was finally squeezing outside of our Kansas front door on cardstock.

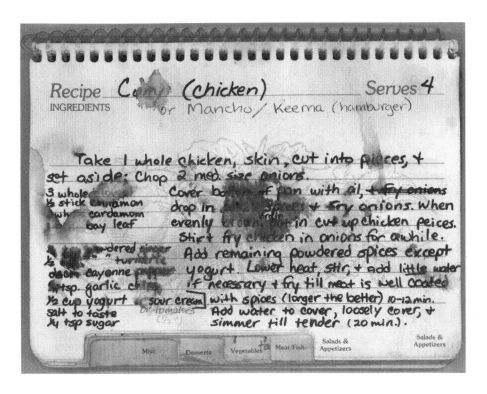

Recipe **C___ (chicken)** Serves **4**

INGREDIENTS ___ or Mancho/ Keema (hamburger)

Take 1 whole chicken, skin, cut into pieces, &
set aside; Chop 2 med. size onions.

3 whole ___ Cover bottom of pan with oil, & fry onions
½ stick cinnamon drop in ___ spices & fry onions. When
___ cardamom evenly brown ___ in cut up chicken peices.
bay leaf Stir + fry chicken in onions for awhile.

___ powdered ginger Add remaining powdered spices except
½ ___ turmeric yogurt. Lower heat, stir, + add little water
dash cayenne pepper if necessary + fry till meat is well coated
___tsp. garlic chips with spices (longer the better) 10-12 min.
½ cup yogurt or sour cream Add water to cover, loosely cover, +
salt to taste or tomatoes simmer till tender (20 min.).
¼ tsp sugar (?)

Misc. | Desserts | Vegetables | Meat/Fish | Salads & Appetizers | Salads & Appetizers

I look at the mix of English and Bengali and smile. Chicken, stew meat, or minced burger would work for this curry, and I have covered my bases. Blots smudge several lines, but I make out "take one whole chicken, skin, cut into pieces and set aside." I groan, remembering my mother pulling at yellow chicken skin over the sink in Kansas, hacking at the carcass limbs. The soft, fatty skin would cling to her fingers and bits would stick to the sides of the sink. She went at the task with a set face, bringing with her from India a sure sense of how things got done in the kitchen. This was odd, though, since she never cooked until after her marriage, until after she was in the United States, really. Meat was not a large part of her diet until then.

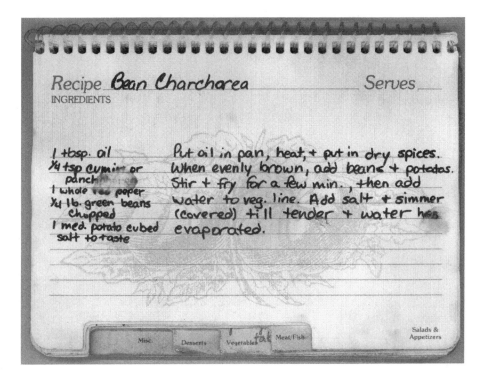

Recipe _Bean Charcharea_   Serves ____

INGREDIENTS

1 tbsp. oil
¼ tsp cumin or
    pinch
1 whole red pepper
¼ lb. green beans
    chopped
1 med. potato cubed
salt to taste

Put oil in pan, heat, + put in dry spices.
When evenly brown, add beans + potatoes.
Stir + fry for a few min., then add
water to veg. line. Add salt + simmer
(covered) till tender + water has
evaporated.

Misc.   Desserts   Vegetables   Meat/Fish   Salads & Appetizers

At our Kansas table, I write, pressing the Flair pen carefully on the cardstock so it won't smear, "Put oil in pan," and I imagine white potato surfaces peeking out from the new-mowed green of diagonally sliced green beans in a china bowl, just off center on my mother's table. She carried my grandmother's insistence on vegetables with her to America. This recipe could be adapted to almost any vegetable—the trick: not to overcook it. I knew vegetables would be a staple in Tunisia with our Peace Corps budget and lack of refrigeration.

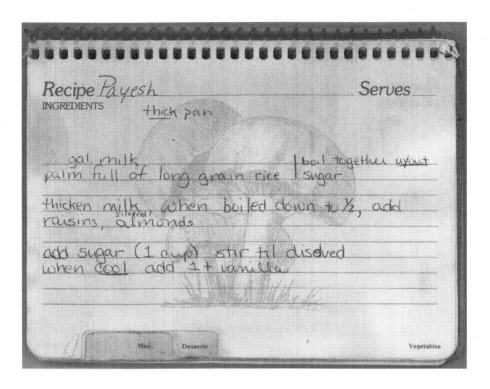

Recipe *Payesh*   Serves

INGREDIENTS   thick pan

½ gal. milk   ⌐ boil together w/out
palm full of long grain rice ⌐ sugar

thicken milk, when boiled down to ½, add
raisins, almonds

add sugar (1 cup) stir til disolved
when cool add 1 t vanilla

Misc.   Desserts   Vegetables

I loved payesh, and, significantly, it did not require the homemade cheese needed to make most other Bengali desserts like sandesh. I did not have to manipulate the chhana into discernible shapes with a particular texture and flavor. I didn't think I'd master the technique before leaving, and payesh was my best shot at making an edible Indian dessert. Plus, my father always asked for payesh for his birthday and I had practice. It wasn't sliceable like cake, but a bowl full of this and all was right in the world. That feeling came to me as I sat with Mom, just by copying the recipe onto the paper; I wanted to have access to that again in Africa.

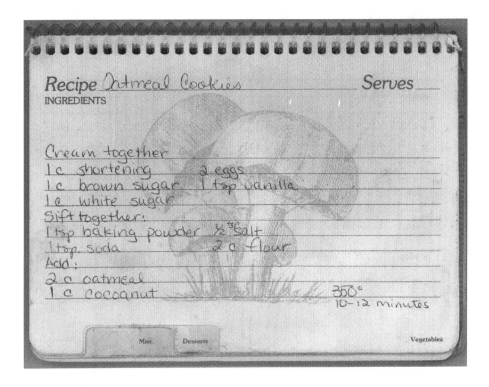

Recipe Oatmeal Cookies   Serves____

INGREDIENTS

Cream together
1 c shortening   2 eggs
1 c brown sugar   1 tsp vanilla
1 c white sugar
Sift together:
1 tsp baking powder   ½ tsp salt
1 tsp. soda   2 c flour
Add:
2 c oatmeal
1 c coconut   350°
                 10-12 minutes

Misc.   Desserts   Vegetables

I decided not to try any recipe prone to melt in North Africa, so oatmeal cookies won out over chocolate chip on the six recipes I took to Tunisia. I didn't think I'd find Crisco in Tunisia either, and my chocolate chip cookie recipe absolutely required one-half cup solid shortening and one-half cup butter, no exception. I would not have an oven there, I knew, but a top-of-burner contraption called a *firma* that was similar to a Bundt cake pan. For two years, my cookies would cook like pan cookies poured in a giant *O*.

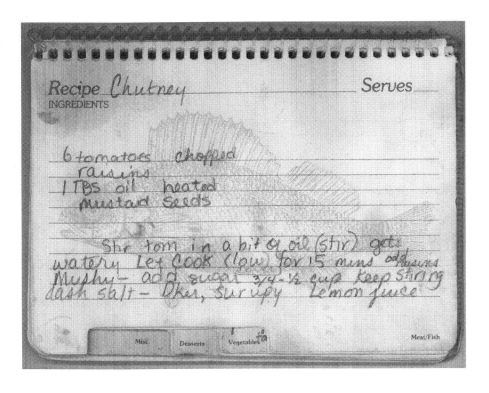

Recipe *Chutney*   Serves

INGREDIENTS

6 tomatoes chopped
raisins
1 TBS oil heated
mustard seeds

Stir tom in a bit of oil (stir) gets
watery Let cook (low) for 15 mins add raisins
Mushy— add sugar 3/4-½ cup keep stirng
dash salt — Okra, Syrupy Lemon juice

Misc   Desserts   Vegetables   Meat/Fish

When I was a child, tomato chutney, bright and soft, was normal to me. Later I learned that most people in Kansas had never heard of chutney made with tomatoes. Even now, the thought of it makes my mouth pucker anticipating the sweet, tart mixture of six chopped tomatoes cooked with sugar, raisins, mustard seeds, and lemon. There are many chutneys, or relishes, in India, but this is a common one in Bengal and in my mother's kitchen. Chutney is meant to cleanse the palate for the next dish, to separate the tastes of lentil and vegetable and meat if it is served, to balance flavors. Whenever I put this chutney on my plate, it runs thickly toward the vegetables.

Recipe **Dal**   Serves

INGREDIENTS Moong┐
            Chola├ types   cumin seed   whole red pepper
            Mosoor┘

1 cup dal   Can add
fill pan 3/4 full of water/boil   carrots early
scoop foam off top + continue boiling   or browned
add turmeric to color + salt to taste   cauliflower late
cook till slurry (add water as needed)   add ginger to
when done: chola while
    heat 2 T butter in fry pan   cooking
        bay leaf — (not for mosoor)
        2 cloves   — use finely chopped onions only
pour in dal
            whole moong cook w/ turmeric /salt /onion —
                    grate ginger 1/4" — simmer
                    take off flame butter 1/2 onion whole red pepper

Moong, chola, moosur, red ones, green ones, yellow, I knew this routine: slowly bring
the pulses to a boil and skim off the surface foam. Add ginger and turmeric, then simmer. Add salt. Later, heat ghee or oil or butter in a small pan, add cumin seeds and
cayenne, and as you pour it on top of the dal listen for the sizzle. As a child, I thought
these lentil dishes always seemed so plain, but before leaving for Tunisia I could not
give up their flavors. I suddenly appreciated their fiber and protein and sensed why
my mother insisted dal was "comfort" food. Cumin seeds were good with moong dahl,
while with moosur, finely chopped onions were tasty. My mother added browned
pieces of cauliflower late in the cooking process to enhance the recipe.

Heritage was so quickly reduced to something I could put in a pocket. Many people have the occasional heirloom vase, photo, platter, or, if they're lucky, a table or two, but the foods we prepare and pass on live in ways the other items cannot because they are adaptable—more cayenne? more garlic, less ginger? My recipe cards are spotted now with water, oil, and tomato drippings, but they can be read, used, and adapted.

In the Indian tradition, I have inherited many fine pieces of jewelry from my family, including a 22-karat gold necklace I dubbed "Cleo" (which was a bridal gift to my mother from my grandfather) because it looked to me like something Cleopatra would have worn, with its gold segmented pieces in a half circle around my neck. There's also a bracelet of my grandmother's with small, finely wrought gold elephant trunks that meet at my wrist, and my grandmother's dangling earrings that cover half my ears. More precious than these jewels, though, are the healthful, delicious recipes my mother gave me. Such a *useful* kind of gift, with the right appeal to my practical midwestern mind; a gift that will not lose value, seem too fancy, go out of style, or get diluted, separated, melted down, or forgotten, even by sloppy keepers of the culture.

MURGI (CHICKEN CURRY)

Serves 4

Take 1 whole chicken, skin, cut into pieces, and set aside (or use boneless, skinless chicken pieces, cut into approximately 1 x 2-inch pieces). One pound cubed lamb or beef can also be used.

2–3 tablespoons oil
4 whole cloves
½ stick cinnamon
4 whole cardamom pods
1 bay leaf
1 dried red chili pepper
¼ teaspoon sugar
2 medium onions, chopped

½ teaspoon powdered ginger, or about 1 inch of fresh ginger root, mashed

¼–½ teaspoon cayenne

¼ teaspoon turmeric

salt to taste

¼ teaspoon fresh garlic, mashed

½ cup yogurt or sour cream or ½ of a medium tomato

¼ teaspoon garam masala (optional)

Cover the bottom of a heavy pan with vegetable oil and heat. When hot, drop in the whole spices and let sizzle for about 30 seconds. Add the onions and stir-fry until the onions begin to brown at the edges. Push them to the side and add the sugar. Stir the sugar in the hot oil until it begins to caramelize and is mostly dissolved. Put in the cut-up chicken pieces. Stir-fry the chicken with the onions until the chicken begins to turn brown. Add the ginger, cayenne, garlic, and salt. Lower heat, add a little water if necessary, and fry until the meat is well coated with the spices (20–25 minutes—this long simmer is essential to bring out the flavor of the finished dish). Add about 1 cup water. Loosely cover the pan and simmer until heated through (5 minutes). Add yogurt, sprinkle a little garam masala into the pan if you have it, and simmer an additional 5–10 minutes. Serve hot.

CHACHCHARI (SPICY GREEN BEANS)

Serves 4

1 tablespoon oil

½ teaspoon cumin seeds

1 whole red chili pepper, dried

¼ pound green beans, sliced on a diagonal (or cabbage or zucchini)

1 medium potato, cubed into ½-inch pieces

½ teaspoon cumin powder

¼–½ teaspoon turmeric

½ green chili, chopped (optional)
salt to taste

Heat the oil in a frying pan. Add cumin seeds and dried red chili pepper, sizzle for 30 seconds or so. Add green beans and potatoes, fry for a few minutes to coat with the spiced oil, then add turmeric and salt. Add green chili if you like. If needed, add a little water to keep from burning. Cover and simmer until vegetables are tender and water has evaporated.

PAYESH (RICE OR VERMICELLI PUDDING)

Serves 6–8

½ gallon whole milk
vermicelli noodles (a bunch about 1 inch in diameter) *or* a palmful of
  uncooked rice
⅓ cup raisins
½ cup slivered almonds or pistachios
¾ cup granulated sugar or ¾ cup palm sugar
1 teaspoon vanilla

In a deep, heavy-bottomed pan, bring the milk to a boil. If you are using rice, add it after about 10 minutes and continue to boil on medium-low heat until the milk has reduced to half its starting volume, being careful not to scorch the pan. As milk reduces, after about 30–45 minutes, add raisins, almonds, and vermicelli if you have not used rice earlier. Add sugar and cook until dissolved, stirring frequently. Remove from heat, cool, and add vanilla (if using palm sugar, do not add vanilla).

OATMEAL COOKIES

Makes one firma (top-of-burner ring-shaped pan with lid), or 2 dozen
  large cookies

2 cups flour
½ teaspoon salt
1 teaspoon baking powder
1 teaspoon baking soda
1 cup shortening
1 cup brown sugar
1 cup white sugar
2 eggs
1 teaspoon vanilla
2 cups oatmeal
1 cup coconut

In a medium bowl, sift together flour, salt, baking powder, and baking soda and set aside. In a large bowl, cream together shortening, brown sugar, and white sugar with an electric mixer or a wooden spoon. Add eggs one at a time and then vanilla. Slowly add in the flour mixture. When combined well, mix in the oatmeal and coconut. Scoop out large tablespoons onto an ungreased cookie sheet, pressing them slightly to flatten. Bake for 10–12 minutes at 350°F.

MOOG DAL (LENTILS)

Serves 4

1 cup moog dal (lentils found in Indian/Asian stores)
1 teaspoon turmeric
1–2 teaspoons salt
1 teaspoon ginger powder or 1 inch of fresh ginger, grated
2 tablespoons ghee (butter or vegetable oil may be substituted)
1 bay leaf
1 teaspoon cumin seeds
1 dried whole red chili pepper
¼–½ teaspoon cayenne pepper

Put dry lentils in a medium bowl, rinse with water, and drain. Wash lentils with at least two changes of water. Fill a heavy saucepan ¾ full (with about 2 pints) of water, add lentils, and bring to a boil. Scoop foam from surface as the lentils cook. After most of the foam is removed, add turmeric, salt, and ginger. Cook on medium heat until a "slurry" forms (add water if needed), about 1 hour. Taste the lentils to see if they are cooked through. In the meantime, in a small pan, heat the ghee, butter, or oil. Add the cumin seeds and the dried red pepper. Sizzle for 1 minute. Take off the heat and add cayenne. Pour over the cooked lentils. Serve hot with rice.

17

Bishshwayya

The recipe cards I wrote that day felt like the sum of what I carried forward into my life from a previous distinct ethnicity. Six pieces of cardstock, small enough to fit in my pocket, were distilled from generations of my family. A month later, armed with my RECIDEX and a sun hat, I set off.

At twenty-two in North Africa, I delighted in giving and receiving hospitality. I had never shared my Indian dishes, as my mother had, outside of my one high school dinner for friends, and yet in the hot Sahara, around a two-burner hot plate in a cement box kitchen, I began to actively shape my food narrative, to give and receive, to relish this exchange of food culture.

Before leaving, I did share other foods, though. For Terry's twenty-fifth birthday, I made my first attempt at a performance cake, one that was showy and tasty. It was our first birthday together and it was cakes that made birthdays in the Midwest, not my family's milk-based Indian sweet, payesh. We lived at Hillcrest Hall in Columbia, Missouri, where Terry was the head resident for the dorm. I was finishing my undergraduate degree at the University of Missouri School of Journalism. It was just thirty-four days after our wedding, and I was primed. I found "Spice Layer Cake with Brown Sugar Frosting" in a dessert cookbook of my mother's. My imagination bloomed with the possibility of spice cake magnificence. However, reality slid its two layers apart in the August Missouri heat as I carried the cake platter across campus for the surprise, resulting in a pool of brown sugar icing dripping messily around the sides. It was like a naked cake with a hoopskirt.

Meals at my husband's German/Swedish family events had distinct traditions, too, and included sweet Jell-O salads that surfaced as green and pink concoctions at the end of a table filled with roasts and chicken, rolls and green beans. Direct from Grandma Sanning to us without mercy, I always thought. Jell-O salad was not in my six cards.

Of course, Terry's clan also produced lovely dishes: beef brisket made to perfection, green beans with vinegar and bacon, mashed potatoes and gravy, Kathy's cheesecake, Susie's sweet potato casserole. They were such good cooks, in fact, that the first time I hosted them after returning from Tunisia I nervously practiced beforehand. In my trial run, I chose roast, thinking it was something they would like even though I had never made one in my life nor ever witnessed such a hunk of meat being cooked. The trial went well. I was shaky but gaining confidence. The day of the party, I carefully pulled off the tinfoil, plucked out the cloves, and poured the onion-soup gravy out of the crockpot. Dry as toast, but my sisters-in-law ate every bite.

There are all sorts of ties between food and family. Every year at Thanksgiving, a local Columbia, Missouri, radio announcer talks about her family's horseradish cranberry sauce, in its fourth generation. She, too, must have lost an elder with an accent, thick shoes, and perhaps German, Bohemian, Swedish, or Irish ways. She, too, is reduced to passing her ancestry on with a recipe. My husband's family has also lost the mores, dress, means of work, language, and, in some ways, the religious customs of their ancestors. It has been a gradual change, like that of the culture in the United States as a whole, not some huge upheaval, like a tooth being pulled, the gum sucking at the lost root.

Through all these changes in culture, my plate did speak to me. No matter where I was, the foods there revealed so much: the landscape from which they came, the trees that fruited, the methods of harvest. For me, India's foods brought to mind vast valleys with square rice fields, drooping trees in hazy heated air, saffron colors of fabric, peacocks, even, strutting in a road. These foods were the stuff of love. "There are people in the world so hungry that God cannot appear to them except in the form of bread," Mahatma Gandhi said. Perhaps this feeling is the origin of the Bengali words like *bhagwan* and *thakur* that applied to cooks in Bengal. I know I do not feel like a bhagwan when I try for the umpteenth time to create my favorite sweet from northern India in order to perfect it for posterity. It's not just that taste I want to re-create, but that feeling of home, of love, of giving, and when I can't quite get it right, when the texture is off, I am lowered somehow. British poet Leigh Hunt said in the early 1800s that bread, milk, and butter "taste of the morning of the world." Food, good food, is indeed the world's morning and a place I wish my family to dwell.

As a Peace Corps volunteer, I was in Tunisia to officially share my Ameri-canness, and I did, revealing a heartfelt love of life, hard work, and generous friendship. But I also shared my Indianness. I thumbed my recipe cards with Mom's five basic Indian recipes. I prepared the vegetable and cumin dish most often. I readily found cumin seeds and powder at the souk. Vendors sat with pyramid-shaped piles of colored spices on boards and I would lean in to sniff one and then another. With my Arabic language training, I could hear the vendors talking to each other, asking "Is she a Tunisian woman?" Then with a glance down at my heavy Rockport shoes and a sniff, "No, she's the American." Arab women, wrapped in safsaris from head to foot, always wore delicate, pretty shoes if they could. With neither an escort nor feminine sandals and safsari, I caused a minor stir. Despite all the speculation about who I was, eventually I found the right vendor and the right spices and took home the carefully poured amounts. I diced potatoes and chopped cabbage or zucchini with no struggle and no strain on our Peace Corps budget.

My Tunisian women friends were an amazing resource; they taught me how to shuck pomegranates, how to fry tomatoes in couscous sauce, and how much cayenne was best, though I had to gradually work up to the amount they liked. They were always so curious about the foods I made that I relaxed to a degree I never had before when talking about India. In Kansas, our food was strange to our friends and no one had been curious. But here, Indian food was treated as a celebration.

At one lunch in Tunisia, however, it was a different story.

My husband's work counterpart, Ali, was coming over. Before he arrived, I snapped a towel as I walked around our living room. The iron bars across the windows of our house didn't guard against the swarms of North African flies and so I adopted this routine to herd the flies into a line that droned outside. Terry ducked as the cloud went past so as not to disturb the flight pattern. To prepare for Ali, I chopped cabbage for *chachchari* to make on the hot plate. I carefully added cumin seeds to hot oil; stir-fried the cabbage; added cumin powder, cayenne, turmeric and salt; I boiled the rice; readied the table.

Ali ate. As I served another helping, he barely broke the motion of his fork to nod in my direction. After eating a plateful he pushed back and said in Arabic, "You've used too much cumin."

Criticism of food so often feels like a gut sneer to all you hold dear. I looked up, and the rough bass note of Arabic began working its way up from my lower throat.

"Oh, you have eaten Indian food before?" I knew he had not.

His eyebrows arched.

"Is it your mother or your wife that does all your cooking?" I smiled sweetly.

I noticed Terry looking at me sideways. As I was annoyed, I began cataloging details. I kept my eyes on Ali, on his stocky build, his light-colored polyester pants with the white shirt pulled tight over a slight paunch at the waistband. His hair was dark brown and pushed straight back off his forehead, his skin a smooth golden brown. I continued in an admiring way, "You have such *strong* opinions about food."

Amazingly, Ali told Terry later that he enjoyed our lunch and that the conversation was very engaging. Perhaps my sarcasm was hard to detect in Arabic.

Once, when we visited a caravan outside the town of Kairouan in the sandy dunes that sweep up from the Sahara, a woman in a woven wool tunic belted with a long, colorful, hand-woven belt beckoned us forward in the Tunisian way, palm down, fingers gesturing toward her torso. She was slightly bent and had striking Berber tattoos on her cheeks and forehead. Her eyes were somewhat filmed. The walls and floor of her tent home were covered in hand-woven rugs, and the interior pulsated with deep red, blue, orange, and cream in dazzling designs. She sat hunched over a coal fire and continued to wave a gnarled hand for us to come over. We sidled up to a large, deep pot sitting on hot coals. Inside was couscous, tinted red with very spicy tomato sauce, and a lone hard-boiled egg lolled in the middle. She pushed the egg, the only protein in the pot, over to us with a large tablespoon. I did not wish to take this from her, from the family of men and women and children that surely would be coming back soon to eat from this same pot. But I had learned the importance of food customs. I was not about to reject her offering or criticize her heavy use of spices. As expected, the couscous was fire-hot. I showed my appreciation in the only way I could: I ate the egg.

When I made lamb curry within two months of arriving in our assigned town of Kairouan, my young friend Samia came over to watch. I had my recipe card for chicken curry or ground meat but lamb was fine, too, and I gamely added potatoes. As I finely chopped the onions, her older sister Hinda came inside, too. Next the three of us cut up the lamb, peeled and cubed the potatoes, and set the whole spices out so they would be ready to add to the hot oil. They didn't wait to be asked but just jumped in and began. The air seemed to swish around their bodies as they moved easily in the tiny kitchen, their hands sure with knives, their eyes inquisitive. The sun was so hot outside that the concrete walls of my shadowed kitchen created an oasis. As we chatted I felt such satisfaction bloom as I did the tasks that I realized that this was what I was meant to be doing. Linking culture with food traditions had gorgeous synergy. I wasn't absolutely sure that the Peace Corps had this in mind when they sent us into the desert, but it connected me more strongly to the women of my neighborhood than did any other job and affected the exchange of culture that the Peace Corps valued so highly. In fact, the women I worked with in town at the Union des Femmes who never cooked with me do not factor largely in my memories of my time in Kairouan. It would take me a few years to find that niche after we returned home to the United States, but find it I did in the food and culture writing and teaching I now do.

As we made the curry, I gasped as I realized I had not cut up enough onion and the oil was getting hot. All activity ceased and a worried frown creased Samia's brow. Then she laughed as Aisha, her mother, bustled in as well with her own knife and shooed me aside to chop. The only pot I had was thin aluminum and meant for the couscous sauce we usually made and I realized it would be tricky to keep a long-simmered curry from burning.

The oil started to let off a stream of smoke and I threw in the whole spices: cinnamon stick, cloves, cardamom, bay leaf, and a dried red chili. The women stood behind my shoulder and murmured a little. I heard Samia shush her sister when she commented that the oil was too hot. Because she was right, I tossed the onions in quickly and stirred fast. Once they became just slightly brown, I added the cubed lamb. I handed the spoon to Hinda. Stir, I said. *Bizzarba* (quickly). A large grin spread across her face.

After the meat browned, we put in the potatoes, the ginger, and then the ground turmeric, cayenne, and salt. I forgot the sugar that day but told them about it, about how a little sweetness added a dimension to the flavor and how the caramelized sugar glossed the onions. We carried on talking and stirring for twenty minutes, then added some water and covered the pan as I turned the burner down as low as possible and crossed my fingers, hoping to let it simmer without scorching until the dish was done. Since I had only the one pot, Samia ran home to get another and I made rice. Aisha smiled and patted my hand when she tasted our efforts. The next day, I was over at their ten-by-ten-foot cement house, a replica of all the others in the neighborhood with its iron grilles on the windows, to help with *tajin* and *lubia*, dishes that I had yet to learn to make.

My project in our Tunisian neighborhood was to make a center for the women to earn certificates in weaving. They were weaving daily anyway, amid caring for children and cooking, but if they had an official certificate, they could earn more for their work. The centers for earning these certificates were all in Kairouan, two kilometers away from our neighborhood of Bourgi. Girls, often taken out of school at nine or ten in the poorer segments of Tunisian culture at that time, were not able to go to town unless escorted. And the men, often, would not do so. I received land from the Kairouan government (which showed Tunisian generosity and faith after I spoke at a town meeting in my halting Arabic and college French, grinning and in effect saying "Give me land"), the cost of bricks from USAID, and my time from the Peace Corps. We built the country's first playground. I took great pleasure in putting together a small slide made to look like a camel. There were tire tunnels and a swing. I negotiated with a contractor to get the building erected. I planned rudimentary reading and math classes to go along with the weaving so the women would be able to read and calculate their bills. The Union des Femmes would conduct the classes after I left. My few photos show this as a dusty corner in a dry neighborhood. But I saw it come together with amazement.

My women friends never discussed my work, though. And my vocabulary after two years centered on words for foods, not construction. No matter that I had successfully gotten an Arab construction worker to pay attention to me that day and get the number of bricks I needed delivered on time, Samia was curious about my tomato chutney.

Chutneys in India, often made from fruit, can be dense. Varieties of mango, apricot, peach, apple, or combinations of these make superb chutney, and fresh mint or coriander chutney are also tasty as savory herbal alternatives. Hot-sour chutney made from lime or even mango is a pungent and astringent option. I didn't think the Tunisian palate would take to the hot-sour taste, but Bengalis savor it and miss its inclusion with meals. Even for me in Kansas, the image of a male relative or friend collecting a bit of lime chutney in a roti and, lips smacking, relishing its flavor to finish his meal was common. The women were always more discreet with food noises. But it was tomatoes that were easy to get in Tunisia.

First, Samia and I heated oil in a deep pan and added black mustard seeds. Once they began to pop, we added six fresh cut-up tomatoes and fried them, then turned down the heat and let them simmer. Since Samia was used to frying tomatoes in couscous sauce, this part did not seem unusual to her. After the tomatoes softened and began to stew, we added sugar and raisins. When the sugar dissolved and the chutney thickened, I took it off the burner and Samia squeezed in the lemon. We put it on the concrete counter to cool. Without refrigeration, it would never be chilled, but she liked the tart-sweet contrast in flavor all the same.

This tart-sweet taste is classic in Bengal and there is a history of it throughout India. As I learned from my mother, the six Ayurvedic dietary tastes include sweet, astringent, bitter, pungent, acidic, and salty. These she included in most meals and I later realized that depending on your own body type and temperament, or *dosha* (humor), certain foods "balance" your system. In many ways, folk culture encouraged the idea that a bit of each of the tastes at each meal, or at the very least over the course of a day or two, would do you good. A spoon or two of chutney took care of two aspects—sweet and pungent.

Samia was not quite as interested in dal. Lentils, though not as much of a specialty in Bengal as in other areas of India, were still a staple in Mom's Kansas kitchen. Dal provided protein and fiber and comforted me on dreary days. Samia's taste buds, like those of most Tunisians, ran to lots of cayenne pepper, so I warned her that my dal was mild, the flavors subtle yet rich. Although she asked to learn how to make it, it wasn't one of her favorites until I added almost three times the normal amount of cayenne pepper to a batch.

It gave me great pleasure that Aisha was happy to share Tunisian traditions with me. And when Aisha heard that our friends Rhonda and Jurgen were coming to see us from Germany, she immediately started cooking. I stopped by her kitchen only to step back out of the way. This was not the day to learn. Every pot the family owned was on the stove or cooling nearby. I watched as she poured five inches of olive oil into a narrow-bottomed stockpot for the couscous. She added tomato paste and fried it in the oil. Then she added tomatoes and continued to fry the mixture. Next, she tossed in onions, garlic, and the beautifully thin-skinned Tunisian potatoes cut in long halves. I marveled at these potatoes, gorgeous and tasty. She had me add chunks of carrots, squash, turnips, spinach, an entire bunch of parsley, a handful of chickpeas, and, because this was a special night, several pieces of lamb. Aisha added garlic, coriander, caraway, salt, and a heaping serving spoon of cayenne pepper (about half a cup). I watched rich sauce bubble under steaming couscous. Then she poured the red sauce laden with olive oil over the partially steamed couscous until it was saturated and tinted red and returned the kernels to steam over the remaining sauce again.

Aisha and her daughters cooked an expansive, delicious meal for us—the couscous, plus fresh French bread from the bakery in town with olive oil and harissa (red pepper paste), roasted sweet peppers, olives, and pomegranates. We ate and laughed for hours—all of the six children; Aisha, with her Berber tattoos etched on her face; her husband, Mohammed, wearing his rumpled wool jacket for the occasion; Terry and I; and our two visitors. Halfway through the meal, I realized that my friends, who spoke no Arabic and little French, were communicating despite the fact that I had not interpreted anything for quite some time. They seemed to get enough information from facial expressions and hand gestures: Mohammed with his palm upraised and rotating, *kul, kul* (eat, eat); Aisha smiling broadly enough to stretch the tattoos on her high and lovely cheekbones; the younger boys watching Jurgen's every move even as they lifted spoons of food to their mouths; Samia, the second oldest, pushing the meat in the central bowl of couscous to the side closest to the guests. Then I listened more carefully, and there it was: our visitors were trying out several phrases in the Tunisian dialect of Arabic. Samia smiled as proudly as a mother when Rhonda said *shkar* (thank you) when more couscous was offered. Jurgen said *bishshwayya, bishshwayya* (slowly, slowly) and patted his stomach, then pushed back his chair and took the offered bowl of pomegranate seeds anyway. Plus, they hesitated only once or twice over the hot spiciness of the food, forever cementing their legend in our adopted family.

There was grace that night. Anytime I was in the kitchen in Tunisia with my women friends I felt it. The women around our modest Tunisian home sensed my openness to their cooking, so they mentored me and watched inquisitively as I cooked. They gently looked over my shoulder, and I felt the air shift behind me as their bodies moved together in our work. Bollywood movies were popular in Tunisia, so in a way, they were predisposed to like foods from the East. They also seemed to like the quiche I made, the oatmeal cookies, and the spaghetti. Mostly, though, I learned from them—I watched and made couscous, tajin, lubia; I shed pomegranates of their coverings and mixed them with cold couscous; I ate olives and harissa. It was in the exchange of food and in the ritual of cooking that I have most of my memories of that time in North Africa. And, hopefully, in my ethusiastic apprenticeship, they have their memories of me.

TUNISIAN COUSCOUS

Easily serves 6

enough couscous for 6 people, about 2 cups dry kernels
olive oil, about 1 inch deep in a large stockpot
1 small can tomato paste
1 tomato, cut into pieces
1 onion, minced
½ pound lamb or beef, cubed (or omit to make it vegetarian)
4–5 cloves garlic, minced
1½ teaspoons black pepper
1 teaspoon salt (or a bit more)
1 teaspoon coriander, ground
1 teaspoon caraway, ground
1 teaspoon cayenne pepper (or more, if you like)
½ cup chickpeas
1 small head cabbage, finely chopped
1 bunch spinach, finely chopped
1 bunch parsley, finely chopped

In a saucepan, heat the oil, put in the tomato paste, and fry for 2 minutes. Add the tomato pieces and fry for 2 minutes, then add the minced onion. Add the meat if using it. Stir-fry until the meat browns and/or the onion begins to brown. Add the garlic and other spices. Add the rest of the above ingredients and enough water to cover. Cook for an hour or so.

Then add the following vegetables:

4 carrots, cut in half lengthwise and then cut into 2-inch segments
2 potatoes cut in half lengthwise and then cut into large pieces

And if you like:

1-2 squash, peeled and cut into chunks
1-2 turnips, peeled and cut into chunks
½ head of cauliflower, cut into chunks

Cook this for another 30 minutes or so. Meanwhile, put the dry couscous in a large bowl and dampen with drops of water. Mix the couscous with your hand until all the kernels are damp. Next, cook the couscous in a couscousier (or a colander inserted in the top of a sauce pot with a lid or a steamer inserted into a big stockpot filled with a couple of inches of water and covered with a lid). Steam the couscous for 15 minutes or so. Place the partially cooked couscous back in the large bowl and pour some of the red sauce from the vegetable pot into the couscous grains. The oil will pour out first and make the couscous tender. Mix well. Put the couscous back over the steam and cover. Steam until tender (probably another 15–20 minutes).

Place the couscous in a large bowl or on a serving platter. Serve the thick, spicy vegetables and sauce over the top of the couscous.

TUNISIAN TAJIN (SPICY FRITTATA)

Serves 4–6

4 tablespoons olive oil
1 pound beef, cut into thin, short strips
1½ tablespoons tomato paste

1½ tablespoons cayenne powder (or to taste)

½ teaspoon salt

1 head garlic, minced

1 teaspoon black pepper

1 teaspoon coriander powder

1 teaspoon caraway powder

½ of a 15-ounce can of chickpeas (or a handful of dried garbanzo beans, soaked overnight)

½ quart water

1 bunch parsley, chopped

8 eggs

½ cup bread crumbs

¼ cup shredded cheese (cheddar works well)

In a heavy pot, heat the oil. Add the meat and fry until browned. Now add the tomato paste and fry for 3 minutes. Add spices, chickpeas, and water and continue to cook for 15–20 minutes or until the water is almost gone. Add the parsley, eggs, bread crumbs, and cheese. Mix well. Place the mixture in a greased deep-dish pie plate or 8-inch square baking pan and bake at 350°F until done (about 20 minutes). The top and bottom should be crisp and the eggs just set. When the tajin is ready, turn it out onto a plate, cut into squares, and serve with a lemon wedge. Variations: Can be made with seafood, or as a vegetarian dish (add green peppers and fresh tomatoes and skip the meat).

TUNISIAN LUBIA (SPICY BEANS)

Serves 4–6

1 cup olive oil

2 cans white beans, or equivalent dried beans soaked overnight

1½ tablespoons tomato paste

harissa (hot red pepper paste available in Middle Eastern groceries)

1 teaspoon black pepper

¾ teaspoon salt

½ teaspoon coriander powder
½ teaspoon caraway powder
½ teaspoon cayenne
water

Heat the oil in a heavy pot. Add the rest of the ingredients and cook about 1 hour over medium-low heat until the beans are tender, adding a little water as needed to keep from burning.

Meat Variations:
When the oil is hot, add ¼ pound cubed beef and 3–4 cloves garlic and brown before adding the rest of the ingredients. Simmer for 1 hour.

When the oil is hot, add ¼ pound cubed lamb. As it begins to brown, add 1 small minced onion. After 3 minutes, add the rest of the ingredients and simmer for 1 hour.

When the oil is hot, add 1 chicken breast, cut into small cubes, and sauté in the hot oil before adding the rest of the ingredients. Simmer for 1 hour.

18

A (Not So) Funny Thing Happened
on the Way to Didu's House

In 1985, between our two Peace Corps years, and thirteen years after my grandparents ventured to the Midwest, I took a midwestern farm boy to Bihar. My dadu came to the airport to pick us up in the cream-colored Ambassador. Terry was along on my family's India adventure for the first time and would soon appear in photos on the rooftop at my aunt's house in the middle of a sea of cousin-brothers and wives, his blond head gleaming. *Jamai* (son-in-law) turned up in photos all over Ranchi, his green eyes and blond hair emerging out of a cotton kurta and loose pants.

At the airport that day, Dadu smoothly pulled away from the terminal at a fast clip, everyone talking. It was curious that the road was so clear of the usual traffic because though Ranchi is considered a town in India, its traffic rivals that of a large American city.

I swiveled my head and saw a propeller plane off to the left and the bulk of the small terminal behind us. Curious, I looked again. Slowly, one by one, those of us visiting—my mother, father, brother, and a friend from Pittsburg—came to the realization that we were not, in fact, on a road. My dadu had ingeniously found a way to avoid some of the hassle of driving in a crowded town by zipping down the airport runway. To this day, I am not sure if he was aware of his daring choice or not. Soon after, with persuasion, my grandfather stopped driving and let the housekeeper's son, Mukund, handle the wheel.

What awaited my new husband at Rani Villa was the *jamai*'s, son-in-law's, welcome into a Bengali family. There is an actual holiday set aside for it in Bengal, *Jamaishashti*, but this was a private affair. The traditional ceremony combines two cherished fixtures in Bengali households: sons-in-law and fish. Fish, especially the fish head, abounds in imagery in Bengal: fish are prosperity, they are fertility, and they are "brain food," ensuring *"khub buddhi hobe"* (you will have high intelligence). Fish is held in such high esteem that at the first rice ceremony of young children, *Annaprashan*, even babies are presented with a cooked fish head (though they do not eat it) for its auspicious nature.

Bengalis come by their love of fish naturally. The entire region of Bengal is covered in rivers, both small ones and major ones like the Ganges, the Padma, and the Brahmaputra. Freshwater fish flourish and so do the recipes for them. My husband's first Bengali fish and official welcome into the family was scaly.

It was midday and an exquisite radiant light filtered the air. There was always such light in my grandmother Rani's dining room, due in part to the high windows, the open, screened doorway, the elevation of Ranchi's hillocks and paddies, and in part to my feeling of delicate rightness there, a keenly felt adjustment of energy. A special pulse converged just there, right at the table where my new husband sat, a broad grin stretching across his face. In that unobstructed moment, all my searching ceased, was unmasked; it had come to this.

I was touched beyond measure when, in the ceremonial way, my grandmother, Rani, prepared a large rui fish. They could have adjusted their ways and just offered him a drink or something. The men could have slapped each other on the back like my dad's Shriner friends did in Kansas when they congratulated each other for some accomplishment. Instead, my family honored us both by simply making the fish head. He was Jamai, American or not, and the presence of the staring eyes on the head reinforced my Bengaliness somehow. Kamla bustled in the kitchen and Rani, wearing a white sari with a wide red border, chuckled as she placed a platter in front of Terry. Rani patted him on the head with a mischievous smile and my mother looked on. My grandfather, brother, and father all sat as Terry now joined the male members of the family. He wore an Indian shirt, a kurta, and told my mother that he was now the favorite son-in-law. The women laughed since this had been my father's joke to Rani all these years. In fact, since my mother had three brothers and I one, they were both the *only* sons-in-law in the family.

The fish head was on the platter and we all held our breath as Terry gazed into its face. Earlier, the jamai had impressed the family by munching on a *chanachur* mix of fried lentils, flattened rice, and hot spices like a born Bengali. The fish head might be a different matter. On the table there was a platter of fragrant rice with a dish of mustard fish and I breathed in the savory spices, steadfastly ignoring the head. There were other favorite foods: *chhanar dalna* (peas and potatoes with fresh chhana), a flavorful *moog dal*, potatoes coated with crushed poppy seeds, and new sweet curds in earthen pots. The creamy top of the sweet yogurt, the mishti doi, would be for Terry. Although Terry was much teased about not diving right into the head, he ate everything, even a bit of the head, with appreciation.

MAACHER-TARKARI (FISH CURRY)

Serves 4

1 freshwater fish
salt to sprinkle on the fish
turmeric to sprinkle on the fish
4 tablespoons vegetable oil
2 medium potatoes, peeled and cut into 1-inch cubes
1 small cauliflower head, broken into 1½-inch pieces
1-inch piece of cinnamon stick
1 bay leaf
4 whole cloves
4 whole cardamom pods
1 dried red chili
1 large onion, finely chopped
½ teaspoon sugar
½ teaspoon ground ginger or 1 inch of fresh ginger, finely grated
¼–½ teaspoon turmeric
¼–½ teaspoon cayenne

1 tomato, cut into quarters

1 teaspoon salt

Wash entire fish, detach the head, and wash again. Sprinkle a little salt and turmeric on the fish head, if you are using it, and set aside. Slice remaining fish into ¾-inch steaks. Sprinkle a little salt and turmeric on the pieces and set aside. Heat 2 tablespoons of the oil in a heavy frying pan and add the potato pieces. Stir-fry for 6 minutes. Add in the cauliflower and fry alongside the potatoes until the cauliflower begins to brown. Lift vegetables out of the pan and set aside. Add 2 tablespoons of oil to the pan. When the oil is hot, place the fish head in the pan and brown on all sides. Remove from pan. Add in the sliced fish steaks. Braise slightly on all sides. Remove from pan. Check pan to make sure there is sufficient oil (add another tablespoon if needed). Add cinnamon stick, bay leaf, whole cloves, cardamom pods, and dried red chili. Sizzle for 5 seconds or until the aroma starts to rise, and add in the chopped onion. Stir-fry onion and whole spices until the onion begins to brown. Push the onions to the side of the pan and add in the sugar. Stir sugar in the oil until it is mostly dissolved. Add the potatoes to the pan and stir. Add the ginger, turmeric, cayenne, and salt. Stirring constantly, fry 3–4 minutes, then add the cauliflower into the mix and continue to fry. Add the tomato pieces. Gently add the fish pieces and head to the mixture in the pan. Add enough water to barely cover the vegetables and fish and simmer until the sauce thickens, the fish is heated through, and the potatoes are cooked completely.

ALOO POSTO (POTATOES WITH CRUSHED POPPY SEEDS)

Serves 4

½ pound potatoes, diced into 1-inch cubes

2 tablespoons posto (poppy seeds)

¼ teaspoon turmeric powder

¼ teaspoon cayenne powder

½ teaspoon mustard seeds

1 green chili, finely chopped (or 1 dried red pepper)

½ teaspoon salt (or to taste)

½ of a medium tomato, cut into quarters

Grind the poppy seeds. Add the cayenne, turmeric, and salt and mix in a small bowl. Add enough water to make a thick paste. Heat oil in a medium-sized frying pan. When hot, add mustard seeds and green chili (or whole red pepper) and let sizzle for 3–4 seconds. Add the potatoes and sauté for 3–4 minutes. Add the poppy paste. After a minute, add 2 wedges of tomato. Stir-fry until the poppy seed paste turns a light golden color and "sticks" to the potatoes. The mixture should be dry when done.

CHHANAR DALNA (CUBED CHEESE CURRY WITH PEAS AND POTATOES)

Serves 4

chhana [see recipe on page 13] from ½ gallon of whole milk, cut into
    ¾ x ½-inch pieces (or buy frozen paneer, which can be found at
    Asian groceries)

3 tablespoons vegetable oil

1 bay leaf

1 dried red chili

4 whole cloves

4 cardamom pods

½-inch piece of cinnamon stick

1 large onion, finely minced (use a food processor if you have one)

½ teaspoon sugar

½ of a tomato, chopped into small pieces

1 potato, cubed into ½-inch pieces

1 cup frozen peas, thawed

1 teaspoon salt

¼–½ teaspoon cayenne pepper

¼ teaspoon turmeric

Heat oil in a saucepan, add cubed chhana, and lightly fry all sides. Lift out of the pan and set aside. Check oil in the pan and add a little more if needed to cover the bottom. When hot, add bay leaf, dried red chili, cloves, cardamom, and cinnamon stick. Let sizzle for 5 seconds and add onion. Stir-fry until onions just begin to brown. Push onions to one side and add sugar. Once it dissolves in the oil, mix well. Add tomato pieces and mix well. Add cubed potatoes and peas. Add salt, cayenne, and turmeric and stir well. Turn heat down to medium-low, cover, add a little water if needed so it does not burn, and continue to stir until the potatoes are cooked through. Add cubed chhana. Heat through and serve with roti or rice.

MISHTI DOI (SWEET YOGURT)

Serves 4–6

1 quart whole milk
8 tablespoons sugar
1 tablespoon plain yogurt with active cultures
2 tablespoons water
earthen pot (optional)
3–4 pistachios, crushed

Heat the milk in a heavy pan. As it begins to boil, add 4 tablespoons sugar, reduce heat slightly, and simmer until the volume reduces by half.

Take the remaining 4 tablespoons sugar and 2 tablespoons of water and heat until the sugar melts and turns golden brown. Add this caramelized sugar to the milk and gradually boil the mixture down for another 15 minutes over low heat. Remove and cool to lukewarm. Pour into an earthen pot or other vessel, sprinkle nuts over the top to decorate, and keep in a cool, dry place overnight. Refrigerate and served chilled.

EASY MISHTI DOI (SWEET YOGURT)

Serves 4–6

1 can evaporated milk
1 can sweetened condensed milk
plain yogurt with active cultures (fill the evaporated milk can to measure the amount)
¼ teaspoon cardamom powder or crushed pistachio

Preheat oven to 350°F. In a medium bowl, mix evaporated milk, sweetened condensed milk, and yogurt using an electric mixer until smooth. Garnish with cardamom powder or pistachios, cover tightly with aluminum foil, and bake for 30 minutes. Turn off oven. Leave the mishti doi in the cooling oven for 5–6 hours. Remove and refrigerate. Serve chilled.

19

Pop Culture India

It was morning in early summer. A recent rain had freshened the air and as I bent over a puddle reflecting sky it was disorienting, like peering into a vast underground, and I jerked back. Nature was enjoying herself. Around me, my Missouri garden unfolded like art. Its point, not a specific outcome but discovery in every moment, drew me into a feeling of suspension.

There is a quality to the places I like: stretched, outside of time somehow. My grandmother's kitchen had that feeling for me. Tiraputi's grand cobbled approach in southern India did as well. I felt the same floating feeling near a clear, ice-cold lake while eating just-caught perch in the Boundary Waters between the northern United States and Canada. It welled up for me at a stop during a bus ride in India when I watched a hungry boy eat bitter peel to reach a banana. Heaven and earth almost touched in those spots and it was not always comfortable or tranquil.

This happened all over the map. Only a few of those moments or the places I remember within their grip happened on officially sacred ground. But I was transformed. That moment in childhood watching the boy with the banana was the impetus behind forays out of my family's pocket of culture to touch the wider world; looking in a puddle in my backyard or taking in the vista of a sound in the Pacific Northwest brought me to myself, woke me up. Just as when I was in the preschool basement in Pittsburg, Kansas, I found that if I was surprised by these shifts, it was by the outside human world, not my own within.

I keep my shoulders on the floor with my hands cupped behind my head and twist so my knee can cross my body and touch the floor. Beside me, my mother, who is visiting my yoga class, begins to giggle. Her elbow has popped up, her knee won't touch the floor, and in general her posture has crumbled. In the background, our teacher intones in a soothing voice, "Do *your* version of the pose." I catch my mother's eye and laugh as the class switches sides.

My version of yoga is sporadic. But I go to classes when I can and on the way there often pass women on the downtown streets of Columbia, Missouri, wearing shawls and long tunics that resemble *selwar kamis*. They are not Indian. I notice again that there is an entire restaurant for vegetarians here, like those I have seen many times in India, and there are vegetarian options on menus posted outside café windows. Hot tea is really hot at corner coffee shops. In my yoga class the day my mother visits, I see the backs of ten or so other yogis in the room. A blond ponytail bounces slightly. No one else in the room is Indian. Indian fabric swags adorn a table at the front and a hauntingly peaceful and faintly Eastern tune plays softly.

Yoga is back, somewhat fierce in its incarnation this time in the United States. The centuries-old exercise signifying mind-body connection has gone mainstream, complete with clothing, mats, tapes, and books to buy. In cities, I note it is sometimes billed as power yoga, which resembles something more competitive and spandexed than the Indian sutras intended. I see magazine ads with celebrities sitting cross-legged, eyes closed with peaceful facial expressions, with headlines such as "just say OM." Om, the Hindu holy mantra that is *not* intended to be something you *do* but a way to reveal who you already are, sounds more like a sports phrase in America.

I hear phrases like "present moment" and "mindfulness" in everyday speech, even among people who do not meditate or do yoga. Not once in all the years in Kansas did I hear people speak like this. There is growing acceptance of Eastern ideas of meditation, especially as Western medical science begins to validate that these practices can reshape our brains and thus, our lives. It fits our culture's good old Yankee independence, somehow: these ideas that spiritual journeys are a rugged, individual experience; that you not only can, but really must, come to spiritual realizations on your own.

On Mondays, I am part of a committed meditation class. I have spent years not talking about spiritual matters, a habit I developed when I realized that my friends in Kansas had as little practice as I did when it came to discussing philosophy. Yet here I am at a meditation class, and I settle onto my usual cushion and look around. I am again the only Indian in the room. But here, most of the meditators have more years of formal practice of my heritage than I do. Many of them are teachers of Vipassana meditation. They spend *time* on this practice, go to retreats, speak mindfully, and rarely judge.

But we all know that cultures have exchanged ideas for centuries. West to East, East to West. The influence of ideas from India, Southeast Asia, and the Middle East has been widespread, though these "new" ways of doing or thinking have not always been attributed to their source. Of course, these ideas mutate in the translation. Americans many times have incorporated yoga and meditation into mainstream culture by emphasizing their ability to transform the body, not the spirituality, of the practitioner. In a sense, many have made these Eastern ideas a marketable commodity here without fully acknowledging their original purpose. Yoga, a five-thousand-year-old physical and philosophical discipline, joins the mind and body together though breath work, or *pranayama*, and postures, or asanas, and includes as components diet, ethics, concentration, and meditation. It is one of the six orthodox philosophies sanctioned in Hindu scripture and later in Buddhist sutras and is used to gain spiritual freedom. Regardless, many times I notice that the image is what's important in the United States. In place of a centuries-old practice of a very individual relationship between teacher and student, we now, many times, have McYoga. But I'll take it. It's comforting to know that people are familiar with your home culture, however tenuously.

There are many ways to love a country. You can love its landscape. Its history. Its ideals. You can love its people. That's what I hear sometimes among travelers. Often, a nation is tested on the *hospitality* of its people, their willingness to give directions, help you find the ticket booth, serve you a meal. Food generosity is keenly felt. At the moment of breaking bread, are you alone in a country or are you in the midst of all its lovely angst, tension, pleasure, and love?

All the ideas I have about country and identity seem to come down to tea water boiled correctly. To warm luchi rolled up with a little sugar. To a boy and a banana. Mine is a gentle affiliation, like many who grew up slightly apart from their origins. Like many with more than one food culture in their families. All of our families are pockets of culture within the larger American landscape. All of us have whole hidden worlds given voice by the food on our dining tables.

After all, what consumes a great deal of the time, energy, and resources of the average citizen in almost any place is food. The identity that binds together the members of a family or community can hinge on religion, clothing, and manners, as well as weapons in times of war. But in significant ways national identity turns on characteristics closer to home: food rituals of ordinary folk.

What does it mean to assert differences between groups of people? We are, after all, one species with surface variations. But we clearly differ in what and how we eat. So the simple act of eating is weighted with complex cultural meanings and is sometimes even the locus of class and political allegiance.

There is a story told by Claire Sponsler in the article "Eating Lessons" of Irish kings who traveled to England in 1394–95 to pledge submission to England's King Richard. A squire was to educate them in the customs of the English, refashioning their behavior from its uncouth state. This squire tolerated their behavior while dining for three days, noting with disapproval that they allowed their minstrels and servants to sit at the same table with them, eat from their plates, and drink from their goblets. On the fourth day, Sponsler says, the squire "had the tables in the hall rearranged and laid in the 'correct manner,' seating the four kings at the high table, the minstrels at a separate table, and the servants at yet another table. This reconfiguration angered the Irish kings, who refused to eat on the grounds that such arrangements were contrary to the customs with which they had been brought up. [The squire] replied that their previous eating arrangement was not reasonable and that they would have to abandon it and adopt the English style, since that was what King Richard wished."

Perceiving that a change in table manners was a necessary accessory to political submission, the Irish kings complied, replicating within the dining hall the larger battles being fought outside as the Irish were being forced under English rule.

Obviously, eating raises the specter of boundary. The link between table manners and subjection in the Irish kings' story underscores the importance of eating as a cultural practice. Manners ratify social divisions. Eating is central. Close to home, the dining table is the court.

Eating and table manners are the mundane, everyday face of our culture—and testing those boundaries with an act as common as sitting down to eat a powerful tool. All my key cultural, spiritual, and family values transferred to me, the next generation, via the ritual around feasting. My cultural identity, which I swore I was losing, passed unnoticed because of the very commonness of eating three times daily. Food showed me how we maintain our differences as well as how we come together.

There is power in food traditions, as well as history. In Bengal, there is lore about taking strength from your local foods, especially before journeys—to "stock up" stamina and wellness until your return. The local soil and water are absorbed into the grain crop, and when consumed, these grains impart their qualities to the people, giving them strength. Historically, in Bengal's villages and towns, food production is linked to monsoon. In wet months, rice and lentils are cooked together to make *khichuri* and served with freshly caught fish. Throughout my childhood, though living in the flatlands of Kansas with no large rivers nearby, nor monsoon, my father often requested khichuri on rainy, cool days, days when he desired stick-to-your-ribs comfort. Mom would cook our largest stockpot full of the lentils and rice and use a large-bowled spoon to scoop out portions. Our plates would hold thick, steaming servings with melting butter or ghee that did indeed comfort.

This attachment bears scrutiny. We are of the earth, grounded to it as nothing and everything else, and the idea that what grows in a region takes strength from it is not far-fetched. The environment in total—soil, air, weather, animal and vegetable combinations, even roads and equipment—create what the French call *terroir*. Terroir infuses the foods from our homelands and creates the taste of home, a taste for which we instinctively yearn.

In an even more intimate way, we take strength from the foods of our family. Our first mouthful was of, or from, our mothers, whose bodies were infused with local foods. The foods later made for us were an extension of that same principle. It is one of our basic lifelong requirements; as food writer M. F. K. Fisher said, "First we eat, then we do everything else." Piece by piece, far and away, the taste of home can be made whole again, or perhaps nothing so much as wholly new.

Yet the art of eating is confusing. The hungry boy who caught my banana and bit through its skin in his haste could have eaten the flesh of the cows that ambled by him, their bells tinkling, or even the dogs, ants, and crickets darting about his feet, if he didn't come from a culture that thinks of these animals and insects as sentient beings. Food ideas are enmeshed in our culture as a result of history, religion, and childhood; enmeshed in our families, in the fact that in my world, Kansans will eat cow but not dog, pig but not horse, the honey secretions of bees but nothing whatsoever from a tick.

There is power in food traditions, but reason? Not as much.

By 1991, after my two children were born, another pocket of culture is reduced now to just one: a new mother with little to pass on to the next generation. I try to weave strands of spirituality and love into food rituals for a growing family, try to pass on thoughts of God by pointing out sunsets to children strapped in car seats. At two years old, Nate points a chubby hand to an orange stripe across the sky because he knows I look for it every day. I say to him, "God is everywhere" and think, *even in you*. Our babysitter comes daily to the house once Anna is born and I am reminded of my own mother's iya in Thailand. I go downstairs to my office to work as they go through their childhood routines until I am free in the afternoon. The woman makes plain spaghetti and noodles, she makes tomato soup and grilled cheese for my babies. I come one day to know that she has also been telling our little girl definite stories of God. Jesus died for my sins, my toddler tells me. I stare into her warm brown eyes and think, *sins*?

We move to the country, a little town, a connected universe, and I finally take the step off what seems like a hundred-foot ladder: I say aloud that I meditate, even to people who have only vague ideas of what that entails. I begin formally practicing faith. I had to will myself to speak of these things aloud but in the end that step off the ladder defines us all. God is great, as they say; he is the ground from which all arises and, as in the teaching of the East, there is no good, no evil, just what is and the judgment we place upon it. It doesn't mean I don't strive for a kinder me, a more accepting me, or that I don't still tend to skirt those less inclined, but there it is. Everything is ordinary and extraordinary. Stepping off that ladder, beginning to practice daily the meditation and mindfulness embedded in the verse of poets, in the world's great religions, in my ancestry, I feel at peace without compass. I try daily to relax into the idea that change happens all the time, the essence of the teachings of Gautama Buddha and also of Kali, the warrior goddess in India, who is fierce and uncompromising. Resisting change is suffering. Nothing remains. All is flux.

My family forged a new branch in this heartland and it is vast, open, and inviting. I write these words, use my hand and my emotions, and it is but the flush of a moment that goes through me. I can allow that in the deep, central place I occasionally discern, its cradling edges teasing and flirting with my familiar world, I am not frozen. There is no permanent truth I can corner. I can step back and see I am at one with the idea that my Indianness is what defines me. It no longer feels like privation to be of two nations.

At this thought, I feel a swell of satisfaction. My children, unlike myself at their age, understand what it is to meditate, that the real work of the world is in individual minds, spirits, and bodies. Even if adjusted to Western tastes for physical exertion and fitness, the concepts of meditation, of yoga, adapt and fit, shift to surroundings. They deepen awareness no matter from which tradition its practitioners emerge.

A feeling of loss gives way to the fact that my heritage has met me on the rebound, unexpectedly in US pop culture, and that my children may have better answers to spiritual and cultural questions than I ever did. And while I might be in danger of losing my language and some of my cultural heritage, my food culture has never been threatened, with or without the ability to make payesh.

In the end, the identifying culture I craved came to me, though not in the ways I expected. It came not in language, nor from formal temple, sangha, or church. It came through food: potatoes coated with crushed poppy seeds, rich carp curry, fiery mustard gravy offsetting the delicate aroma of freshwater fish, sweet mango chutney to cleanse the palate before a last course. It rises to meet me in aroma, in a world of recipes, in a pocket of culture that fits exactly right. If I wanted, I could open a new earthenware pot of sweet curds and reserve the creamy top for the man of the day, or for my own jamai. A series of sweets in their delicate syrup, and payesh, the very king of desserts, is mine, and yours, for the making. The cultural baton is stretched out, clasped, however gingerly, and passed on.

Over the years, I have added to my repertoire of six recipes that I took with me to Tunisia: coconut shrimp, mustard fish, sour-hot chickpeas, pungent vindaloo, black-eyed peas with mushrooms, eggplant dishes, dishes with yogurt sauce, and more. I have improved at cake baking. I concoct a favorite shortbread cookie dipped in chocolate. But it is always the elusive dish I seek. I knead my last batch of sandesh and produce again brittle balls for the effort. This time, though, I pour the pieces into a bowl of payesh—creating what my mother sweetly claims is an authentic, sought-after variation of the king of desserts, and in fact the crumbles taste wonderful—soft, even—in the muddle.

CHHANAR PAYESH (SWEET THICKENED MILK WITH CHEESE CUBES)

Serves 4–6

chhana [see recipe on page 13], cut into small cubes

½ gallon whole milk
small bunch vermicelli noodles, about 1 inch in diameter, or a palmful
    of white rice
⅓ cup raisins
½ cup slivered almonds or pistachios
1 cup granulated white sugar or 1 cup palm sugar
1 teaspoon vanilla

In a deep, heavy-bottomed pan, bring the milk to a boil. If using rice, add it now and continue to boil gently until the milk has reduced to half its starting volume, being careful not to scorch the pan. As the milk reduces, after about half an hour, add raisins, almonds, and vermicelli. Add sugar and cook until dissolved, stirring frequently. Remove from heat, cool, and add vanilla (if using palm sugar, do not add vanilla). Add chhana cubes (or in my case, crumbled sandesh pieces). Enjoy!

RAINY-DAY KHICHURI (RICE AND LENTILS WITH VEGETABLES)

Serves 4–6

2 tablespoons vegetable oil
1 bay leaf
(1) 1- to 2-inch stick cinnamon
4–5 whole cloves
4–5 whole cardamom pods

1 cup rice

1 cup dal (I like moog dal best, or moosur)

½ teaspoon turmeric

½ teaspoon cayenne, or to taste

1½ teaspoons cumin powder

2 teaspoons salt, or to taste

water to cover dal and rice (about 2½ cups)

1 potato, peeled and cut into chunks

½ cup peas

1 cup cauliflower pieces

1 teaspoon dried ginger powder, or 2 teaspoons ginger paste

½ of an onion, thinly sliced

1 teaspoon cumin seeds

1 whole dried red chili

2–3 tablespoons ghee (or butter)

Wash rice and dal in several changes of water. Drain. Heat 1 tablespoon of the vegetable oil in a heavy stockpot. Add bay leaf, cinnamon, cloves, and cardamom and let sizzle for 3 seconds. Add rice/dal mixture to the hot oil. Stir to coat. Add turmeric, cayenne, cumin powder, and salt. Cover the mixture with water, add potato pieces, and cook over medium heat with a lid slightly ajar. After 25 minutes, add in the peas and cauliflower pieces. Continue to cook another 20 minutes, then add ginger. In a separate small saucepan, heat the remaining 1 tablespoon oil and when hot add the sliced onions, cumin seeds, and red chili. Stir-fry until the onions are light brown. Add this mixture to the khichuri. Next, in the same saucepan, heat a generous 2–3 tablespoons of ghee (or butter) and add to the khichuri to flavor.

Special variations: add ¼–½ pound of peeled, deveined shrimp to the pot while cooking. Beat 2 raw eggs in a bowl, drop in, and stir well after the khichuri is done and still piping hot.

Serve with Indian papper (crispy thin pepper-crackers found at international food stores), fish, eggplant, or any other vegetable chachchari.

❖ ❖ ❖

PORK (OR BEEF) VINDALOO

Serves 6–8

1 tablespoon cumin seeds
4 dried red chilies
1 teaspoon black peppercorns
½ teaspoon cardamom seeds
1 teaspoon fenugreek seeds
1 teaspoon black mustard seeds

1½ teaspoons salt
½ teaspoon sugar
4 tablespoons white wine vinegar

2 tablespoons vegetable oil
1 large onion, finely chopped
2 pounds boneless pork shoulder, or 2 pounds lean stewing beef, cut
    into 1-inch cubes
1-inch piece of fresh ginger root, peeled and grated
4 garlic cloves, crushed
2 teaspoons ground coriander
½ teaspoon turmeric

1½ cups water

Grind the first six spices into a powder. Add salt, sugar, and white wine vinegar
to make a thin paste and set aside. Put 1 tablespoon of the oil and all of the
onion into a food processor to make a coarse paste and set aside. Heat the
remaining 1 tablespoon of oil in a large pot or wide frying pan. Add the cubed
beef or pork and stir-fry for 10 minutes. Remove the beef from the pan. Put
the onion mixture in the pan and fry for 5 minutes. Pour in the vinegar and
spice mixture and stir well. Add ginger and garlic and continue to stir-fry for
2 minutes. Add ground coriander and turmeric and fry for 2 minutes. Add

the beef or pork back into the pan and mix well. Add 1½ cups water. Cover and simmer for 1 to 1½ hours or until meat is tender.

BAEGOON BHARTA (EGGPLANT WITH ONION, TOMATO, AND SPICES)

Serves 4

2 large eggplants, 1 pound each
1 tablespoon vegetable oil
½ teaspoon black mustard seeds
1 bunch spring onions, chopped
3 garlic cloves, crushed
1 red chili, finely chopped
½ teaspoon cayenne
1 teaspoon ground cumin
1 teaspoon ground coriander
¼ teaspoon turmeric
1 teaspoon salt
(1) 14-ounce can chopped tomatoes, or the equivalent amount of fresh tomatoes
2 tablespoons fresh cilantro, chopped
lemon juice to taste

Wash eggplants and wipe dry. Puncture eggplant skins with a fork and rub a little vegetable oil over them. Bake in 400°F oven for 1 hour or until soft. Remove and cool. In a heavy pan, heat the oil. When hot, fry the mustard seeds for 2 minutes, add the onions, mushrooms, garlic, and chili, and fry for an additional 5 minutes. Stir in cayenne, cumin, coriander, turmeric, and salt and fry for 3–4 minutes. Add the tomatoes and simmer for 5 minutes. Chop each eggplant, including skins, and add to the saucepan. Add fresh cilantro. Bring mixture to a boil. Reduce heat and simmer for 5 minutes or until sauce thickens.

Acknowledgments

My heartfelt thanks to my family, Terry, Nathan, and Anna Furstenau, and my parents, Sipra and Sachin Mukerjee, who make everything possible.

I thank and appreciate my writing friends and mentors who helped shape my work and perception: Maureen Stanton, Marly Swick, Sandra Scofield, Gretchen Henderson, Ann Briedenbach, Jen Gravely, Laura McHugh, and others who have encouraged me to be the writer I am today. To my friend, Beth Hand Johnson, who, unbelievably, can remember the first poem I ever wrote, and to Anne Robinson, for her generous friendship, I send gratitude, always. I thank the Vermont Studio Center for their gift of time and marvel still at the group of amazing writers and artists I met there. I thank, too, my editor, Catherine Cocks, and the University of Iowa Press for all the work they do so incredibly well.

The epigraph comes from Mary Oliver, *House of Light* (Boston: Beacon, 1962), 32–33.

A portion of the prologue of this book appeared in *Painted Bride Quarterly*, Print Annual 5, titled "Biting through the Skin."

Recipe Index